ORDINARY HEROES

ORDINARY HEROES

The Journal of a French Pioneer in Alberta
by Marcel Durieux

TRANSLATED AND EDITED BY ROGER MOTUT AND MAURICE LEGRIS
WITH AN INTRODUCTION BY L.G. THOMAS

The University of Alberta Press

First published by
The University of Alberta Press
Edmonton, Alberta, Canada
1980

ISBN   0-88864-069-2
copyright © The University of Alberta Press   1980

Canadian Cataloguing in Publication Data

Durieux, Marcel.
    Ordinary heroes

ISBN   0-88864-069-2

    1. Durieux, Marcel.   2. Frontier and
pioneer life—Alberta.   3. French in
Alberta—Biography.   I. Motut, Roger.
II. Legris, Maurice.   III. Title.
FC3672.1.D87A3   971.23'4'0924   C79-091226-0
F1078.D87

Printed by
Hignell Printing Limited
Winnipeg, Manitoba

This edition and translation of Marcel
Durieux's journal is dedicated to the
memory of the French farmers who helped
to settle Western Canada

Contents

Foreword

Marcel Durieux, one of the first settlers to become established in central Alberta, was born in the French province of Hainaut (now a part of Belgium) in 1889. His father, Charles Durieux, having suffered serious financial reverses, decided to emigrate to Canada. Thus, in the summer of 1906, Charles and two of his boys—Henri, twenty-two, and Marcel, sixteen—made the long crossing by boat to Montreal and, then, the other lengthy trip by rail to Winnipeg. There, after consulting with people in the land office, they decided to try their luck in the Red Deer district of Alberta. By October, they had established themselves a few kilometres west of the village of Big Valley, some thirty kilometres south of Stettler. They were joined the following year by Madame Durieux and their third son Jean. The family and its descendants remained on this site for many years, although the parents died in 1910 and the Great War claimed two victims: Jean, killed in the Battle of Verdun, and Marcel, so seriously affected by poison gas that he was never able to return to Canada. The farm was later abandoned as insufficiently productive.

Such heroic French names as La Vérendrye, Thibault, Lacombe, Grandin, and DeSmet are commonly associated with the discovery and settlement of the West. However, the role of the ordinary French farmer in this work has gone pretty well unnoticed—although, as this journal amply demonstrates, even the "ordinary" settler had to have some heroic attributes merely to survive. Yet, survive he did; he may not have prospered to the point of becoming affluent, but he was at least able to gain enough from the often tough and recalcitrant soil to encourage his continued residence on the land he had first broken. There were others, of course—Swedes, Norwegians, Ukrainians,

Germans, Americans. However, the role of the French in settling central Alberta is not only of historical importance, and, thus, worthy the emphasis this journal places on it, but of humane importance as well. This account is one of how people from one land went to another far-off land, which their ancestors had helped discover and explore; how they helped one another, with patience, simplicity, good humour, and charity; how they assisted their neighbours, of whatever nationality; and of how, at long last, they saw their heart-breaking labour produce food.

Seen in such broad terms, it's not a new story, certainly. The same general account has been written of different peoples and places for centuries. But, given this specific time and setting—central Alberta at the turn of the century—this simple story becomes important, in spite of its simplicity, as an almost archetypal element of the cultural and social history of Western Canada in general and, specifically, of the role in Alberta's history played by the French settlers.

Although it is true that many of the early Western-Canadian settlers, woodsmen, and travellers kept journals, it is equally true that few of the works that have so far come to light are of much value, either historical or literary. The journal of Marcel Durieux—here translated from the French and edited—is an exception. Durieux was a farmer, not a man of letters; yet, his journal is clearly the work of a man who was both sensitive and intelligent. He was acutely aware of others: their sufferings, their unspoken hopes, their loneliness. He was unreservedly loyal to those who befriended him and willing to help them at whatever cost to himself. He was intensely affected by the land-scape, especially the sharp and deep canyon of the Red Deer River, which he could see from his cabin window, and its long hills rolling away on both sides. He was profoundly religious, although his feelings in this regard were expressed very simply, almost matter-of-factly. In short, Marcel Durieux appeared to be just another of the hundreds of hard-working, long-suffering farmers who first broke the prairie; yet, as these pages testify, he was very much aware of himself as an intellectual and moral being. It is for these reasons that his journal is worth being printed, read, and preserved.

The editors of this journal, anxious to see if anything remained of the house built by the Durieux family in 1906, tried to find the site in July 1978. Beginning at Stettler, one hundred kilometres east of Red Deer, we went south on Highway 56 for about thirty kilometres to the village of Big Valley, passing by Lowden Lake, which Durieux mentions several times. We also made a side trip on secondary roads in order to find other sites mentioned by him; thus, we passed by Ewing Lake and the Ewing Post Office, which had, long ago, once been a one-room schoolhouse. Directions given to us by a friendly farmer, Monsieur Gendre, who was acquainted with the history of the Durieux family, even led us to the Chapel of the Immaculate Conception, well hidden in a grove of trees not far from Ewing. This small, solidly-constructed church appears not to have been used since the 1930s, although a fresh coat of exterior paint showed that someone still cares for it. At the rear of the church, we found a framed letter from Monseigneur Legal, in which the famous Bishop gives his permission to the church at Ewing to construct the stations of the way of the cross; the letter is dated 1911, at Saint Albert. An old cemetery nearby contains a number of French graves; judging from the dates of death, some of these people may well have known Durieux in those years between his arrival in Alberta and his departure to engage in World War I.

Then, after having searched in vain for the Durieux farm for several hours, we were finally directed to its approximate location by a local farmer. We reached it, however, only after having left a country road and having cut across a number of fields, their bumpy nature evidence enough that they had not been tilled for many years. Having reached the old house, we immediately realized that our troubles had been worthwhile. Their home was magnificently situated: it stood at the bottom of a long but gently sloping hill, with a flat plateau stretching in front of the house for about two hundred metres. This plateau ends in a sharp, steep drop to the valley of the Red Deer River, the river itself being another two hundred metres or so beyond. The west bank of the river, for as far as one can see, is a high, almost sheer cliff. The east side continues as we have described it for another three to five kilometres, at which point the valley abruptly ends and is replaced by the same sort of high, steep cliffs as on the west side. Thus, what the Durieux family saw from its front door were the plateau, the cliffs, and the valley plain on the east side; the river; the steep cliffs on the west side;

and, in the distance, the high, narrow canyon of the river. On all sides, stretching back from the river and its valley, are long, gently-rolling hills. It is one of the most striking, beautiful prairie views we have ever seen.

The Durieux home is still standing, although one half of it was removed years ago to add to another building on a nearby farm. It is a small house that seems even smaller because of the grandeur of its setting; no other human habitation can be seen for miles. One who knows the history of this home and of the people who lived in it—kind, courageous, strong morally and physically—examines it with a profound respect, remembering that, years ago, a small group of bewildered strangers came here, built a house hardly bigger than a modern garage, and, then, barely managed to suffer through a savage winter. The house is decaying rapidly, although what we thought to be the original wall plaster is still evident in places. There are signs of what was once a garden, and there are a few relics of farm machinery and part of a runner from a heavy, horse-drawn sled.

The farm has been abandoned for some time, since the land is not strong enough to produce good crops consistently. The only inhabitants now enjoying the awesome view are birds and rodents. Yet, to anyone who has read Durieux's journal, this place will be imbued for years to come with the memories of the French farmers who gave their lives to the soil.

The editors wish to thank Mrs. Jeanne Goloski, of Fort McMurray, Alberta, niece of Marcel Durieux, and Mrs. Alice Labonne, her mother, of Three Hills, Alberta, for their encouragement and for having provided us with some old pictures of the Durieux homestead.

Marcel Durieux's manuscript is a continuous narrative; the chapter divisions and titles have been added. The editors have tried to make their translation as faithful as possible to the spirit and the style of the original. Thus, the reader may notice some inconsistencies, such as the use of both kilometres and miles, as well as some unusual phrases and expressions, there being no graceful English equivalent for the original French.

Roger Motut and Maurice Legris

Introduction

  As the colours and lines of the western Canadian mosaic are dimmed and blurred by the passage of time and the fading memory of the pioneer, the recovery of this account of the experience of the Durieux family in rural Alberta between 1906 and 1914 assumes a peculiar significance. The Durieuxs were French, and the settler from metropolitan France has been little noticed by the historians, both "academic" and "popular," of western Canada. The impression that is often left is that France was a country with no surplus population for export and that her people, in any case, had little disposition to emigrate and even less to adapt to the barbarities of a primitive, Protestant, and predominantly Anglo-Saxon environment.

  The Durieuxs do not fit readily into this stereotype. They were middle class, accustomed to a high degree of material comfort, literate, devoutly Catholic, and conscious inheritors of a great cultural tradition. Indeed, they had rather more than a fair share, by egalitarian standards, of those attributes that might be expected to render emigration unthinkable. The elder Durieux, Charles, seems to have been, like many other emigrants of diverse nationalities and very different circumstances, decisively influenced toward leaving France by a conviction that western Canada, and particularly Alberta, could offer his sons an opportunity to escape the constrictions of an established society in which he had suffered serious material reverses. As his son's manuscript makes clear, all his friends and relations did not share his views. His friend Musy's highly unfavourable view of Alberta may, however, reflect an attitude to the Canadian West more widely held in Quebec than in metropolitan France. There, the manuscript hints, the sense that life in Alberta could mean high adventure may have touched at least the informed *bourgoisie,* as it certainly had similar circles in the British Isles and Germany. Marcel, the author, was, he admits, a reluctant emigrant. It was his older brother Henri, perhaps significantly the only member of the family to return to Alberta after the War of 1914 and to remain there for the rest of his life, who seems to have been the prime instigator of the enterprise. Yet, as it turned out, it was Marcel, only seventeen, who bore with his father the brunt of the earliest stage of a homesteading experience that began in October of the year 1906, not long before the beginning of the winter of 1906-07, not one of the mildest in central Alberta's history.

The Durieux ability to adapt to the harsh conditions of pioneer homesteading cannot easily be questioned. Though little is said of financial matters, it does seem clear that they were, in spite of serious losses in France, cushioned, rather more firmly than the homesteader of popular imagination, by the possession of some means. There are the familiar complaints of the emigrant about the appalling conditions on immigrant ships, but the complaints are admittedly made from the relative comfort of second-class passage, to which the Durieuxs were relegated by the fact that there was no first-class on the S.S. *Pomeranian.* Though they ran short of food supplies, this was more the result of bad weather and long distances than lack of money. They were able to purchase stock and implements, to hire needed services, to pay for medical treatment, and to purchase an additional half section to add to their homestead holdings. These things could not have been done out of the returns on their land and stock in the first early years. The Durieuxs, though by no means rich, were obviously neither penniless nor improvident. Indeed, there is a reference to "a welcomed inheritance" that allowed the purchase of ten calves to use the large quantity of hay the Durieuxs put up.

The Durieux family, in this sense, were "privileged" among the homesteaders. Yet, their adjustability to new ways is illustrated by the circumstances under which the original homesteads were taken up, when Marcel, then under age, registered in the name of his older brother Jean, unable to join his family until the completion of his military service a year later. This, scarcely within the letter of western Canadian land regulations, was done at the suggestion of a young Rhinelander, cheerfully avoiding his German military obligations, with whom Charles Durieux had struck up an acquaintance while awaiting the arrival of his sons in Red Deer—they had been left on Manitoba farms to gain experience while their father made a reconnaissance of homestead prospects in central Alberta. The experience of Henri and Marcel with their farmer employers seems to have been distinctly happier than that reported by youths from not dissimilar backgrounds in Britain.

Possibly, a French middle-class background produces fewer inhibitions about class than a similar background in late Victorian and Edwardian Britain, but the Durieuxs, both the older and the younger generation, seem to have been blessed with an ability to get on with people of all kinds, a useful ability under pioneer conditions. Their response to the Finnish log cabin and its occupants suggests that to the Durieuxs cultural difference was more interesting than offensive: "never again was it given to me to admire such an interior. Imagine . . . a rectangle made of tree trunks, superimposed and carefully made weather-proof with moss . . . the whole thing roofed with split spruce logs covered with dirt!" The same adaptability enabled the Durieuxs, after some initial misgivings, apparently prompted by not altogether good-natured gossip, to make friends with their two English neighbours, Seymour and Freer, who in other contexts, one may suspect, might have been stigmatized as remittance men. Here, possibly the genteel reached out to the genteel, but certainly the Durieuxs overcame any inhibitions aroused by the austere image the two ranchers presented to some of their neighbours.

The Durieuxs' adaptability, so apparent in their meetings with the great variety of fellow settlers, had a practical side. Though the senior Durieux might have been unwise in disregarding the advice of a seasoned carpenter in the insulation of his house, he and his sons met the problems of countering its icy draughts by exploiting a nearby seam of coal. Though they took serious risks in this amateur enterprise, they showed, here as in their culinary efforts, a truly Gallic sense of the importance of creature comforts.

The Durieuxs, in common with many pioneers, whether settled as individuals or in groups, found comfort in association with those of a similar ethnic background. The French-speaking community of Alberta, small and scattered as it was, especially to the south of Edmonton, was overwhelmingly from eastern Canada rather than directly from metropolitan France. One is sometimes left with the impression that the vast majority and the small minority quickly developed a kind of francophone equivalent of "No Englishman need apply." There is no evidence for this here. The Durieuxs appear to have been on friendly terms with a large number of French-speaking individuals and families, and to have felt a solidarity with them, whether they were French or French Canadian, Belgian or Swiss. There were French-speaking groups in the vicinity of several central and southern Alberta points, among them Pincher Creek, High River, Calgary, and the Durieuxs' own town of Stettler. Perhaps the most conspicuous group, in this period of rapid development for Alberta between the turn of the century and the outbreak of World War I in 1914, was the colony, mostly of former military officers, at Trochu, to which Marcel makes reference. The Trochu group, with its preoccupation with horses and its ambitious schemes for development, was rather grander than anything near Stettler. In politics, the Trochu settlers were extremely conservative, even reactionary, whereas there are at least hints that the Durieuxs were more moderate in outlook and would not have seen eye to eye with their aristocratic compatriots on such touchstones of French politics as the Dreyfus case.

The importance of the support of the French-speaking community to the Durieuxs, and its solidarity, is dramatically illustrated by its response to the most tragic events in the Durieuxs' Canadian experience, the deaths, within a matter of weeks, of their parents. Madame Durieux, whose health had steadily deteriorated, died after an operation in the General Hospital in Edmonton. At her funeral in the cathedral, only her doctor, two nuns, and a nurse attended, except for her son Marcel and her husband. When the broken-hearted Charles, in spite of the diversion of a planned journey to France, died scarcely three weeks later, more than thirty people from the French community were at the church and the cemetery to offer their sympathy in this double loss.

For the French community, the church was a rallying point, and, for the devout Durieuxs, it was a constant in their relationship with the new and in many ways strange world to which they had committed themselves. The manuscript makes many references to attendance at mass, wherever they happened to be. The Durieuxs played an active part in the building of a Roman Catholic church in Stettler, and, being musical, they played the organ and sang the solos for a choir Marcel describes as "some sort of melting pot of the Catholic world" of this part of Alberta. The clergy, necessarily itinerant because of the scattered nature of their flock, played a major part in keeping the Catholic and French-speaking settlers in some kind of community relationship. The centrality of the churches in mitigating the loneliness and uneasiness of what was essentially an immigrant society was something of which the Durieuxs were fully aware. Their apparent ease in establishing relationships with their polyglot neighbours was perhaps as much related to their deep attachment to their faith as to their comfortable acceptance of cultural difference.

Compared with the homesteader who had no resources beyond his own strength and determination, the Durieuxs may be seen as especially privileged settlers. They had at least a modest reserve of capital, a better than average education, and a degree of sophistication that, with their native shrewdness, protected them from exploitation. They came to a country whose history and development had been profoundly influenced by the French presence, at a time when tensions between the two founding peoples, if not resolved, had relaxed to a point where a French-Canadian prime minister could command a majority in the House of Commons and solid support in the West. The Durieux experience, in spite of the tragic death of the parents of this devoted family, suggests that they had no difficulty in developing a sense of place in a society whose structures were a cause of uneasiness to many in the multitude of new arrivals. By 1914, the three brothers, and the wife of the eldest who had just arrived from France, appeared to be on the high road to success.

The outbreak of the War of 1914-18 was a shattering blow to Alberta. This was the most lately settled of the provinces, and one whose institutions, rapidly improvised, had had no opportunity to solidify into a reliable structure. The proportion of the young men of military age who were recent arrivals from the British Isles was high, and enlistments from this group were especially notable. The Durieux brothers, in a corresponding position as nationals of another major combatant power on the Allied side, hastened to return to France. Jean was killed. Marcel, a victim of poison gas, spent the rest of his life in France. Only Henri returned to live out his life in Alberta.

  The heavy casualties of the First World War drastically affected the structure of the age group in Alberta, which might have been expected to provide the leadership of the middle years of the twentieth century. Of those who survived, many did not return to Alberta. Many of those who returned had been transformed, even shattered, by their experience. If they came back to Alberta, it was no longer the buoyant and self-confident province of the pre-war decade. Pockets of optimism and determination survived but "the last, best West" faced an uncertain future. Readers of this manuscript may well ponder what the loss of people like the Durieuxs, and their potential influence, may have meant to the French presence in Alberta.

L. G. Thomas
Professor of History (Emeritus)
The University of Alberta

I

Ultimate act: the departure of the immigrants

A small station, long and flat in the night. A narrow, wooded valley under low clouds. My father, my brother Henri, and I are standing on the platform. We have just arrived from Amiens and are awaiting the train to Le Havre. Tomorrow, we shall board a ship and cross the Atlantic for the New World. We are supposed to dock at Montreal. On one of the benches, a station employee is half asleep. Henri, who is always curious, leaves the station to return half an hour later, rather disappointed.

"It's dark out there! Like an oven; . . . I couldn't even see the houses in the hamlet, . . . and to think that the place is called Clères [Clear]!"

We find room on a bench and sit there with our suitcases. At the end of the concrete platform where the baggage car will stop, there are two lonely wicker trunks. These constitute our worldly possessions, and, as I glance at them, I cannot help but think, this is truly a picture of the departure of emigrants.

Before us lies the future; . . . for me, it is nothing but a big, black hole. Behind us, a whole world of memories makes me feel terribly depressed. As far as I am concerned, being only sixteen years old, I feel no enthusiasm whatever. I am abandoning a career in which I was interested, and, moreover, I hate moving and changes of all sorts. I also know that our departure is being interpreted as an escape. It is Henri, especially, who pushed us into this expedition. Mother followed, and father, after five years of struggling, finally admitted defeat.

Last night when we left Somain, the only persons on the station platform to see us off were Madame Villette, a close friend of my parents, and her daughter Henriette, who was about my age. Monsieur Villette will meet us at Le Havre. We shall travel to Le Havre via Paris, but we can't visit Paris because we haven't the means. My mother, who is very tired because of the events of the last few weeks, is in Belgium with friends, and Jean, my other brother, is completing his military training. Last night on the station platform, Marie-Henriette was like a fountain of tears; . . . I almost found it indecent. It was I who should have been crying, . . . and, yet, I held back the tears, . . . but it seems to me now that I am getting smaller and shrinking between Henri and my suitcase on this bench.

At Le Havre, however, things picked up. Mr. Villette had treated us to a meal at a famous restaurant, in order, said he, to help fight the forthcoming seasickness. I filled myself as much as I possibly could. When the time came around for cigars, I am sure that it wasn't the smoke that filled the eyes with tears; dad and Mr. Villette were very old friends and were never going to see each other again.

I do not mean to slander, and I am sure that the now defunct Allan Line won't be troubled, but I must state that the S.S. *Pomeranian* was nothing but an old shoe. S.S. in English must stand for *sale sabot* [sloppy shoe]. This boat was nothing but a vulgar cargo ship and should never have been allowed to take on paying passengers. This, however, was the time when Canada wanted to fill its solitudes. Organizations, which, after all, didn't want to spend too much money, took it upon themselves to bring, to Montreal in summer and to St. John or Halifax in winter, a flow of immigrants. Immigrants travel in one direction only. The company solved the problem of the return trip by transporting live cattle from Montreal to England [refrigerated cars did not exist at the time]. We were human freight used by the company to complete an insufficient cargo!

Our last gesture of pride had been to take a second-class cabin. There was no first class (one can understand why!). This allowed us to endure (if that is the proper word) the endless crossing. Furthermore, it gave us free access from stem to stern, and we were able to judge for ourselves as to what was meant by third-class passengers. Human decency and respect for my title of man forbid me to enter into details on the subject.

Some day, someone, I hope, will research and describe these horrors.

The S.S. *Pomeranian* was still tied up when a sick person was discovered on board: she was a young blonde woman from Roubaix, accompanied by her two brothers—the Frères.

In spite of all this, we found ourselves to be among the fortunate ones aboard. We occupied one of the permanent cabins in which there were two superimposed bunks. I had to sleep on a small cushioned bench, so that, when the wind hit the stem and we started to pitch, I was often emptied from my improvised bed. But, there was a porthole and fresh air. In the temporary sections, there was only one porthole for every three cabins.

When our boat, pulled by two tug-boats (one on each side), left the docks, there were very few parents and friends to wave good-bye. Once again, we were among the fortunate, because Monsieur Villette walked faster and faster on the jetty as our speed increased. At the end of the channel, our friend stopped running near a small lighthouse, but we saw him for a long time, waving his hat at the end of his cane. . . .

Soon, the increased swell off the coast seemed to become more accentuated, and so did that feeling of being very small, . . . which I had experienced on the station platform at Clères. The copious meal of Le Havre was not long in joining the fish, . . . although Henri and my father weren't bothered at all and, in fact, had struck up a conversation with some of the passengers.

That night was really awful for me. My empty stomach seemed to twist in pain in the sweet, smelly air between the two decks. In the morning, I hurried up to the open air of the spare deck where I felt much better. What really cured me in the afternoon was a full glass of champagne that a fat, tottering gentleman thrust into my hand. Without even thinking as to what the effects might be, I swallowed the whole thing in one gulp. A few minutes later, I was out, . . . and, one hour later, my sea-sickness had disappeared.

The blunt stem of our "shoe" plowed through the greenish waves of the Atlantic with difficulty, while, on our right, huge capes seemed to rise in an almost unreal way. We were having our last look at the British Isles. We then passed a small flotilla of fishermen, and, finally, the ocean spread out before us! We had finally left the old country.

I did not have to be a maritime expert to notice that, with a head wind, the *Pomeranian* advanced at about five knots, and that, with a tail wind, its speed could at times double. When the wind was really strong, it pushed our boat along at a speed double that which could be reached by the engines. On a really good day, we could travel four hundred and forty kilometres, but, even then, after eight days, we were barely approaching the Grand Banks of Newfoundland. In order to gain time, it had been decided that we would navigate the strait between Newfoundland and Labrador. It was 10 July, and the ice-bergs had begun to drift down from the north. Each night, a sailor plunged a small receptacle into the ocean to take the water temperature. During the night, our speed was cut still more as a wise precaution.

Life on board continued rather monotonously, especially for the young lad that I was. The meals, because of the type of cooking, were a real chore for us. Even the coffee, much appreciated by people from the northern countries, was a horrible mixture. A rather plump nun, superior of some order, tired of the food, asked for a simple potato salad each day, but was never able to get it. There was neither oil nor vinegar on board. She was offered, instead, pimento, cinnamon, nutmeg, cloves, ginger, mint, powdered celery, four types of pepper, pieces of cauliflower in mustard, dill pickles, and, finally, the ever-present catsup! The only food we did enjoy was the fruit and jam pastry . . . and the tea, in which we poured twice as much hot water, because it was really strong.

On the night of the ninth day, the wind direction, which for a week had held a steady west-by-north-west direction, changed to north-north-east. This forced our cargo to adopt a sort of oblique position, a little like that of a dog trotting sideways. We gained two knots. There was a full moon, and the watchman on the stem and above the top deck could easily have seen the white mass of ice-bergs had there been any. The next morning, the dot indicated on the marine chart impressed us. We had moved much more rapidly. Water was really churning behind the propellers, and our wake was clearly marked by two foamy tracks that spread toward the horizon. When, by chance, we met a boat whose stem was raising high sprays, we didn't appear so helpless, because boats, like everything that moves, have their own personal characteristics.

One morning, three blasts of a sharp whistle caused us to turn and look. An enormous two-toned grey silhouette could be seen in the rays of the rising sun. Immediately, the officer in charge gave three blasts of our ship's whistle, and we felt the *Pomeranian* slide toward port. Under a trail of smoke, the oncoming liner majestically split the waves, and, soon, it filled our horizon. Our deck was full of people, yelling, screaming, and waving. Over there, on a gigantic ship that passed us without effort, not a soul was stirring—only those three huge stacks belching smoke. We were being passed by the latest creation of the Hamburg Amerika Linie, the *Bremen.*

Yet, the stubbornness of our small ship was admirable. Way down below the decks, in the hold, huge boilers and an intricate number of machines were steadfastly at work, activating the four blades of the propeller. From all parts of the ship, night and day, we could feel the pulsation of vertical cylinders that suddenly speeded up when the propeller came out of the huge waves. As we had a good cargo on board, we didn't roll too much. Three enormous bronze bells loaded at Le Havre and destined for the Lac Saint-Jean region were part of our cargo. We also had much machinery from Birmingham, England, which was going to Montreal and Toronto. On the other hand, in a head wind, the rolling proved hard on this relatively short boat. The waves would hit the stem from underneath, and, as the load was in the back, the little *Pomeranian* would almost stand straight up; . . . once the crest of the wave had been passed, it would plunge straight down into the hollow while, up above, the propeller spun in the air.

That afternoon, the weather turned much cooler and a strange spectacle appeared before us. All of the horizon seemed dotted with black specks equally spaced. A sailor, who spoke a little French, explained to us that these were small fishing boats from Newfoundland. We didn't see them for very long because a thick fog started to engulf us. In one-half hour, it was pea-soup thick. The furious whistle started to blow from minute to minute. Toward evening, our progress was practically nil. Soon, the engines stopped completely. What a spectacle! Every thirty seconds, everyone would jump at the strident screech of that whistle, and we could see unhappy looking people around us, some of them even scared. I thought about the small boats out there and what had become of them. Our captain was careful, but there were other boats whose blasts we could hear, which either passed us or crossed our path. Sleep was impossible in all that howling. Only during the day, between two fogbanks that weren't quite as thick, would the ship move again, and it seemed that we were also fighting a current that came at us from an angle.

The noise lasted three days and nights. When we were able to check our position again, we noticed that our boat had drifted six hundred kilometres toward the south-west. In the beginning, our course had been set to the north of Newfoundland. Neptune had decided otherwise. Joy returned to all the faces when a magnificent sun, dissipating all the clouds, allowed us to catch a glimpse of a long, irregular coast-line on the horizon. We found out later that those far-away peaks belonged to a mountainous chain in Labrador. We were destined to see a great deal more of bush and rock before reaching the promised land.

We travelled all night and woke to discover another coast-line on the other side. We had penetrated into the Saint Lawrence estuary. Soon, we passed a charming island and were told that it was the property of the Menier brothers. Finally, a small welcoming bay came into sight, bordered by pretty villas decked up with fluttering flags. There were French flags flying. But why?

"It's the fourteenth of July!" someone cried out.

The *Pomeranian* itself was flying the tricolor on one of its masts. On shore, people were waving at us. We had reached Rimouski. Our boat reversed its propeller, and, at the same time, a pilot boat approached from shore. A rope ladder was thrown overboard, by which two solid fellows from the small boat climbed onto the *Pomeranian*.

We were now floating on calm waters between two magnificent shores. The pilot was busy guiding his ship. We crossed other heavily-laden boats, which indicated to us that Canada had a lot of merchandise for exportation. The rising tide was helping our progress, but the dimensions of the topography here were so great for us, Europeans, that we appeared not to be moving. On our left, from behind a low hill, we suddenly noticed a long trail of smoke, and, as the land flattened, a red and black, serpent-like train appeared. We could hear its whistle echoing across the water, "Choooo! Choooo! Choooo!" to which the *Pomeranian* answered. How much brighter all this was than the Newfoundland fog!

Ahead of us, a boat that appeared to be a transatlantic was belching torrents of smoke. As it passed us, we had to crane our necks to see its pilot. It must have been six stories high; ... yet, in this immense vastness, it almost resembled the small ferry-boats on the Seine. New perspectives opened before us on all sides, so much so that we didn't know where to look. This wonderland went on until nightfall. The boat slowed down until it almost touched the steep banks of an island, . . . the anchor was lowered, and a small craft took a tow-line to shore where huge posts were sunk into the water. Navigation at night was too dangerous on the river.

The next morning, the engines woke us before sunrise. Our little *Pomeranian* was finding it difficult to fight the current, until the rising tide caught up with us. Now, the shoreline was much closer. There were no more islands. On the right, a large bay appeared, and overlooking a harmonious amphitheatre stood a city clambering up the flank of a hillside. A ferry-boat broke away from the dock, and we could see its enormous paddle-wheels covered with foam, glittering in the sun as it crossed in front of us. Its deck was loaded with vehicles of all sorts: buggies, wagons, and even a few automobiles whose passengers waved handkerchiefs or hats at us. At the same time, a tug-boat was coming to meet us. It passed us on the right, circled around, and came up on our port side. The pilot from Rimouski left the ship to climb down onto the smaller craft where he shook hands with the captain. We were gradually pushed in toward the docks where strangely dressed dockers secured the *Pomeranian* in no time at all.

There was an air of strangeness about all this. The quays were deserted—the long cranes weren't moving and the railroad yards were quiet. We remembered that this was Sunday and that, here in Canada, work ceased. We obtained permission for a three-hour shore leave, and both Henri and I set foot for the first time on the soil of our new country: Canada. This was a momentous occasion for us, and we were both aware that, over three hundred years ago, another Frenchman named Jacques Cartier had dropped anchor somewhere close by, impressed by the sights before him. In a few moments, we were on our way to discover Quebec city!

It would take too long to recount in detail all we did in two and a half hours. We climbed from the lower town to the promontory above, and, as we passed in front of a beautiful church, hearing hymns that were so familiar to us sung in our own language, we entered and thankfully attended the last part of a mass—five thousand kilometres from home! We then marvelled at the Chateau Frontenac and its huge tower, and, for two more hours, we literally devoured the streets of this beautiful city, . . . until familiar whistle blasts from the *Pomeranian* called us back. Upon reaching the ship, we suddenly realized that we hadn't eaten, and as we devoured a cheese sandwich father teased us by quoting an old northern French proverb: A donkey who does as he pleases has already received half its pittance.

That night, we docked at Trois Rivières, and, before dawn, we were on our way on the last lap of this endless odyssey: Montreal.

II

Arrival on the Prairies

When the ship docked, Henri and my father were seated on our trunks and I was seated on my suitcase.

"This time," said father, "there will be someone to greet us upon our arrival. Naturally, you don't know my old friend Alfred Musy, and I haven't even a photograph of him to show you, but, for the past three months, I've spoken to you about him, and he knows you through my letters. If he hasn't changed, we will be welcomed, but be careful. Although he is a very kind man, he can be rudely blunt because he has his own fixed ideas about things. I know already that he is not pleased that we should go west. Alberta, according to Musy, is an impossible country and he believes it to be a crime that Europeans should be sent there. We will let him talk, and, after ten days of a cordial visit, we shall discreetly leave for Red Deer where I should find some of the passengers who were on the ship with us. I also have the addresses of the land office and French families in central Alberta. Friend Musy is an engineer who graduated from Polytechnique; he started his career in the Cail Establishment where you worked as an apprentice one and a half months ago, Marcel. As he had specialized in sugar refineries, he first went to Egypt to install equipment for Cail and then to Cuba, Puerto Rico, and, finally, Virginia, where he decided to work for American companies. He ended up in Maine where sugar beets are refined, and, as the distance from Maine to Montreal is not very great, on one of his visits he met his present wife. They now live at the Sault au Recollet and have four children."

"How long has it been since you last saw your friend?" asked Henri.

"Something like twenty-two or twenty-three years."

"And how old is he now?"

"He must be well into his fifties."

"Twenty-two years! That's a long time. He's probably changed a lot and won't be easy to recognize, . . . and you probably have changed too."

By this time, two tug-boats signalled that they were coming alongside. They pushed us like they were big shepherd dogs, made us turn around, almost on the spot, and edged us through pilings until we almost touched a dock marked Allan Line. On our left was the S.S. *Ionian* (that I was to know so well in 1914). We found ourselves overlooking a huge hall where hundreds of people from Montreal were massed. This must have been some sort of way of spending time for them! Rolling gangways were brought up, and immigration officials climbed aboard to sit at portable tables on the deck. Passengers were sorted into line-ups.

"Please, have your passports and your money ready," a man with a loud voice shouted in English and French.

Those who hadn't the required sum of money were turned back. Another announcer repeated the same thing in German, a Slavic language, and Polish. While father stood in line, Henri and I tried to discover our friend in the mob below. People were shouting at us:

"Want a good hotel?" "How was your trip? . . . Do you want to rent a farm not far from Montreal?"

Meanwhile, Henri was carefully and methodically scrutinizing each zone in this huge room. Suddenly, he grabbed my arm and with his other hand indicated an area on the left.

"I'll bet you that's our friend Musy!"

"You're crazy," I said, "you never saw him. How can you be so sure?"

"See that big man over there with a white suit and panama hat? He's inspecting every face up here!"

The man below was impatient. He shoved another man out of his way. I ran to father in the line-up and pointed at the character down below.

"Well, I'll be . . . but of course. . . . That's him all right!"

We all shouted his name. . . . He had seen us, and we heard him bellow.

"Charles Durieux!"

We were finally leaving this old *Pomeranian*. It wouldn't be the last time we mentioned its name, however. After the first handshakes and introductions, it wasn't long before Mr. Musy let us know his ideas about western colonization.

"Charles, I tell you this. It's a rotten shame for a civilized government to organize the immigration of poor European beggars and send them to regions that are uninhabitable!"

As Henri was about to open his mouth, my father put a finger to his own lips as if to tell us that arguments wouldn't help.

The Musys lived at the Sault au Recollet, and we got there by street car. Mrs. Musy was a charming person, and her children thought that I was a real hero because, one day while trying my luck at target shooting, I shot and hit a lump of earth that the little girl had thrown into the air. We were also introduced to Mrs. Musy's relatives and were given a real briefing on what the West was like. The brother-in-law knew a fellow who had been a trapper out there and who always had to carry a rifle with him. The uncle was ready to bet that we wouldn't last two years out there, where winters last for eight months, . . . and one can barely harvest potatoes, . . . and where the wheat freezes in August, . . . and where the hail storms are horrible . . . egg-size. . . . Yes sir! There were cyclones, too, and houses were known to fly away like match-boxes. No roads, no bridges, . . . and railroads hundreds of miles away!

Dad tried to show them official documents as well as letters from persons who were already out there, but, try as he might, for these people of "Bas Canada," all of this literature and propaganda was nothing but a big bluff in order to provoke a "boom."

"My dear friends," my father resolutely said on the night of the fourth day, "we are truly thankful for your kind hospitality, but we did not change continents to remain in Sault au Recollet. Tomorrow, we shall be on our way by CPR for Winnipeg, where I shall secure the latest information from the land office about Alberta. During my stay in Alberta, Henri and

Marcel will be placed on farms in Manitoba to learn something about their new life. When I have found good land, I shall have the boys join me and we shall build our home."

Mr. Musy thought my father crazy and said so in no uncertain terms. He reminded dad that we were now in mid-July, that winter was at hand, and that there wasn't time to do all the things that had to be done, . . . and his list was long! He suggested that father leave us in Montreal and go out there alone to find out for himself. Father wouldn't be moved.

The next morning, after breakfast, we were ready to leave. We could tell that Mr. Musy was not happy at all. The parting of the two old friends at the station was rather cold, . . . and they were never to see each other again.

The Canadian Pacific Railway coaches were spacious and comfortable; their locomotives, however, were noisy and huge. We settled down in our Colonist Car with its bunks that could be lowered or raised above the windows, and, before we knew it, we felt ourselves moving out of Windsor Station. At each end of the coach stood a small stove that kept water boiling almost constantly. There was ice water in a fountain, for drinking, and the washrooms were very clean. However, if the coaches seemed perfect, the rail-bed wasn't at all the same once we had travelled beyond Ottawa, and what had been an almost straight line now became a series of ever-winding curves that followed the terrain. Happily for us, we had been warned about the endless regions of rocks, spruce trees, and lakes. We noticed that the crew had changed twice and that two squares had been removed from our tickets.

The next day, at dawn, we were already at the windows. We were still rolling in the same desert of rocks and stunted trees. We didn't speak. I could see my father, tight-lipped and frowning. Henri had assumed a detached air, . . . and all sorts of thoughts went through my mind. What if Mr. Musy was right? Around ten o'clock, on the left, a huge body of water was shining, and, as we followed its coast-line an hour later, it seemed to me that I could see a ship on the horizon. We were told that this was Lake Superior. After two hours along its shores, we were beginning to get tired of looking at it. For eighteen days, we had seen nothing but water!

At the next round-house stop, we were given two locomotives. This was to overcome a steep climb that brought us back to that eternal lake. Until nightfall, the same kind of country continued on and on. I was beginning to get fed up, especially the next morning when more of the same appeared. We had completely lost the notion of time, and our watches had to be set back one hour. We even forgot to eat our bread, cheese, and water. Since our departure from Sault au Recollet two days before, we had not had a hot meal, the stoves being continuously used by a group of Slavs who kept on drinking gallons of tea. I assure you that my morale was low after having spent the second night in that hard bunk. After all, what had we seen for two thousand kilometres if not rocks, rocks, and more rocks . . . and trees and water? Would Mr. Musy be right? All at once I remembered the sadness of my young friend Henriette on the station platform of Somain. Had she confusedly felt with her child's instinct that we were heading on an expedition doomed to fail? I would see the look in Mr. Villette's eyes when he left us at the Havre, a look full of regret and compassion. . . . If, at the next stop, some all-powerful person had climbed aboard and invited us to turn back, I think that I would have jumped at the opportunity! Then, monotonous hours without sleep went by. We stopped in a town whose name must have been Indian. It was two in the morning, I was cold, and I couldn't sleep. I was desperately trying to make sense out of all this. Could it be possible that, one day, statesmen had this railroad built leading to nowhere? This railroad represented a gigantic investment of funds and human effort, almost superhuman, and, surely, it was not with the aim of fooling a poor, innocent people like all of us. It just could not be! There must be something out there in the West that was worth all this effort!

The day was breaking behind our train; our third day since Montreal. I climbed down to join Henri and dad, who were already looking out the window. I peered out and shouted almost simultaneously.

"Look! There's grass out there!"

"And there are cows too—look!" Henri added, surprised by my excitement.

As daylight increased, we noticed a few farmsteads where oats were swaying in large fields, . . . and, later on, we saw our first wheat field. Things were improving in our coach, and there was new interest on every face. Finally, we could spot large grain elevators, and dad told us that we were entering the city of Fort William. We arrived at the station and took advantage of our stop to eat. We were able to buy a can of corned beef and biscuits. To our great astonishment, the biscuits were salted. . . . It was our first taste of soda biscuits! Anyway, it was better than bread and cheese, and, to mark our arrival in this promising country, we even had a bottle of beer.

The train was now able to travel faster. The country-side was gradually changing, and, during the day, we left Ontario and entered Manitoba after passing another large expanse of water known as Lake of the Woods, where coquettish villas lined the lake and people, who appeared well dressed, waved at our train. If this continued until we reached Alberta, we would certainly have a good one on Mr. Musy! Toward the middle of the afternoon, we entered the suburbs of Winnipeg, the metropolis of Western Canada.

In 1905, Winnipeg was already a fair-sized city. It was spacious and clean, with imposing buildings and monuments. Its stores were well stocked, especially the T. Eaton and Company store, where one could find anything from a safety pin to a threshing machine or grand piano. We were interested in locating the land office. Dad wanted to find out about home-stead land in Alberta and find a place for the two of us to stay while he travelled there alone.

The Immigration and Land Office Building favourably impressed us. Its architecture inspired efficiency and solidity. Inside, we found pleasant, polyglot employees who led us to the proper offices. Really, we did not feel like objects that were being exploited anymore. These people really tried to make us feel at home. On the walls, there were huge maps of the three Prairie Provinces. Indicated in white were lands that were still free, and other colours showed lands already taken, according to the year they were occupied. In Manitoba, there were few white zones; in northern Saskatchewan, the immaculate zone was very large; and, in Alberta, everything was white but for a few tentacles of colour here and there.

The agent pointed out the Red Deer region on the map. It was half-way between the cities of Calgary, the most important centre in Alberta, and Edmonton, which had just been designated as the capital of the new province. At the time, Calgary was on the CPR line, while Edmonton had no east-west railroad, . . . but it wasn't far, because, according to the map, the Canadian Northern Railway was approaching the city from the east. There was a railroad from Calgary to Edmonton and a branch going east from Lacombe, which stopped at Stettler. That's where father decided to go.

We were then escorted to another office responsible for the placement of apprentice-farmers on Manitoba farms. The name of a man in Somerset, an area in the south-western part of the province, was given to us. On the map, we noticed that, when father would be in Stettler and we in Somerset, the distance between us would amount to something like seventeen hundred kilometres! We had a lot of trouble adapting to the vastness of this huge country.

A French Canadian, whom we met on our way out, happily created a diversion to the sombre thoughts invading our minds. He invited us to visit St. Boniface, a small city across the Red River from Winnipeg. There was an important hospital administered by a religious order there, as well as a prosperous college near a beautiful cathedral. My father rented rooms in a modest boarding-house operated by a Frenchman who had fought in the war of 1870. This created an immediate link between these two old veterans, and, in spite of that terrible war, they seemed to regret the passing of the "good old days." Our father, who was fifty-six years old, had been a prisoner of war and had gone through a great deal of physical and moral pain, contracting chronic bronchitis in the Coblentz camps. Henri and I used to smile at these war stories, which seemed a mania for these veterans; . . . little did we know that, thirteen years later, we too would be veterans and that young people would smile at our own stories.

In the St. Boniface restaurants we found a cuisine quite different from that of the *Pomeranian*. The American influence, with its tomato sauces, mustard, and hot sauces, was evident here. The bread, butter, and milk were plentiful and excellent. The pastry resembled that of Alsace and Lorraine, . . . but we had to drink tea or coffee. All the liquor in the world could be found here, but at prices out of the range of our budget.

Our morale was pretty low when time came to say good-bye at the CPR station in Winnipeg. It was a very beautiful August day, and we had to appeal to reason and courage at the moment of separation. Henri and I were leaving for a civilized area; we were young and healthy, but, for dad, it was different. He was on the threshold of old age and leaving alone for an unknown region. The sinister predictions of Musy were playing on my imagination. Father sensed our worry and said, almost as in a prayer:

"My children, we all are in the hands of God, . . . and I am sure that your mother's prayers are with us at this moment."

III

The problems begin

After six hours of travelling and one change of trains, we did find a poor French farmer at the Somerset station. He declared that he could only take one of us. In Winnipeg, we had been told that we would be together, and Henri tried to convince him of this, but the old man, who was tall and skinny, would not change his mind. However, he consoled us by saying:

"Don't be alarmed, my children. I saw old man Boignot in town a while ago and he said that he would like a hired man from the old country to help with the hay." We met the old Auvergnat and he agreed. I went with the tall man and Henri with the Auvergnat. How strange it seemed to us hearing these two Frenchmen in the heart of Western Canada, speaking in their native accents. The tall man looked at me and said:

"I'll give you one dollar per week. Agreed?"

I glanced at Henri, who made a sign that I should accept. I did, and asked:

"Are we going to be far from each other?"

"Well, there must be almost five miles, but you can spend your Sundays together," replied the old man.

At this, Boignot added:

"For the big brother, it will be five dollars a month. Those are starting wages, but you will have room and board."

The deal was settled, but, when the time came to load my suitcase on the wagon, . . . there was no box! Old Louis (that was his name) had delivered a load of logs in town. There were only the front and back log bunks held together by a narrow board. I had to tie my suitcase as best I could so it wouldn't fall off.

We had barely left the small town when the road disappeared to give way to an unforgettable track. It wasn't bad on the prairie, but, when we crossed freshly-cut bushes, there was nothing but a succession of treacherous stumps that we couldn't dodge. I had little to hang on to. After about twelve kilometres of this exercise, my body ached all over, and it was with relief that I heard the old man announce:

"Well, my boy, we're home."

In a hollow between two partially wooded hills, a log cabin appeared. Our team had been heard, and out of the cabin came a woman in her forties, a tall, thin girl in pig-tails, and a sturdy-looking, red-headed fellow who spoke first, in the speech of a French Canadian.

"Hello! I see you've got the greenhorn! Don't look too tough to me! What's your name?"

I introduced myself.

"What kind of work did you do in the old country?" he persisted.

"I was a draftsman and worked on locomotive plans," I answered drily.

This answer left the fellow stunned, but for a moment only. He burst out laughing and, slapping his thighs, said:

"No wonder your arms are so thin!"

Everybody laughed. . . . I asked old Louis:

"Is that man your son?"

"No, he's a fellow I hired in the spring; he comes from Quebec. . . . Come now, lend a hand, mother, and untie his baggage and show him to his quarters upstairs."

Turning to me he added:

"You'll sleep with Gaudias."

Thus did I learn the fellow's name.

"And you, Marie," he said to his ragged-looking daughter, "you help Gaudias with the horses while I feed the stock."

When I entered the house, I noticed a lack of cleanliness, and, up there in the attic, which was to be my sleeping quarters, only an Indian blanket separated Marie's room from our own. This loft appeared to me to be a more sordid place than any Rembrandt could ever paint. Nothing was missing in the tableau. The permanent light and shadows and haphazardly hanging rags in a background of dust and cobwebs made fantastic garlands. Our common bed was wide and the mattress soft. In spite of the fact that there were no sheets, the blankets were clean, the top one being an assortment of a thousand pieces somewhat reminding me of Arlequin's robe.

While I unpacked, Mrs. Louis went down to prepare supper. When I came downstairs, I noticed that there was only one room. It served as dining room, kitchen, and bedroom for the old folks. However, Mrs. Louis had cleaned very appetizing-looking vegetables, and the odour of good soup floated up from a venerable-looking pot that must have come from the old country.

My services were required to carry water, and, as night was approaching, I noticed that, when my two hands were busy with the water pail, millions of mosquitoes buzzed around my head and landed on my face and neck. Then, it was the wood pile. For the first time in my life, I was introduced to the bucksaw (later I would become an expert at handling this instrument).

The setting sun, flamboyant in carmine and gold, coloured the fragile trunks of birch and poplar groves. Between these, a beautiful field of ripening oats undulated in a light breeze, and, in a clearing toward the north, a rectangular flowering wheat field was closed off by a line of dark trees on the horizon. Toward the east, there were sloughs and clumps of willows and poplars in a natural prairie where long, shiny grass glistened in the sunset. In spite of the mosquitoes, the charm of this very quiet spot comforted me in my loneliness. I had feared that Western Canada, from the literature I had read, would be nothing but a monotonous plain void of trees and hills. The thought struck me that when old Louis had prospected for a place four years ago, in spite of his rough aspect and his disrespect for cleanliness, he must have been very sensitive to beauty, and this was a beautiful site. When, later at the supper table, I mentioned this to him, he eluded my question by displacing it.

"My boy, when you meet your brother at the Boignots, you'll see something much more beautiful. There are trees and hills and a small river out there which winds under a railroad bridge.... It's really something to see!... But, for farming, there is a lot of wasted area between the creeks and the cutbanks."

As I felt in a teasing mood and old Boignot had been mentioned, I said:

"Seems to me that old Boignot is a bit of a penny-pincher?"

"Oh! He's not so bad. He pinches pennies, I suppose, like everyone else; ... his wife is a very good woman, ... but they have Auvergnat ideas when it comes to medicine."

"Would he be some sort of a quack?"

"Oh no! He never tries anything except on his own family, . . . and it's a good thing because their eldest son probably died because of that attitude."

I looked so astonished that he continued.

"I don't mean to say that the old man killed him, ... but, when his son had a shot-gun accident, they let him bleed to death because they thought that blood-letting would help!"

My goodness, I thought, I hope nothing happens to Henri. . . . What if they were to let him bleed if something happened? Old Louis must have read my thoughts, because he added immediately:

"Now that the other son is married to a French-Canadian girl, he hasn't the same ideas as the old folks, ... and the young people know what the good remedies are."

We finally got down to eat, and I must admit that Mrs. Louis knew more about panhandles than broom handles!

After supper, Gaudias interviewed me about mechanical drafting; the explanations I gave plunged him headlong into comments.

"You surely won't find that kind of a job in Alberta!"

He went on to add that Alberta was a place the good Lord had forgotten, and, that when my "old man" would write to me, it probably would be to tell me that he was coming back. Well, thought I, another one to comfort me about Alberta.

Then it was Marie's turn, who, with her moody face, began to quiz me about the life of young girls like herself, in France. I had started to tell her about it when old Louis brusquely interrupted and said that it was time to go to bed, because tomorrow we had a lot of hay to cut.

I was so wrecked and tired that I slept like a log next to Gaudias, who didn't move any more than a stone in the bottom of a well. In the morning, I was awakened by Marie as she rattled down the stairs. We went out to feed the stock while Mrs. Louis prepared the porridge into which she mixed chocolate; . . . it was the only culinary concession that she admitted. While the dew was slowly disappearing, I turned the grindstone handle to sharpen the mower blades.

Until noon, the two horses pulled their noisy, clickety cart in and around hollows where a wild mint fragrance filled the air near the willow groves. Gaudias drove the horses, while old Louis, with his scythe, cut the strips between the bushes where the mower could not penetrate. With hayforks, Marie and I spread the thick bunches of hay so they would dry more normally. Right up until nightfall on Saturday, we mowed, coiled, and hauled hay to the large loft in the barn (cleaner than the one we slept in). We also made two large haystacks in a small pasture nearby.

On Sunday morning, I wrote my father and addressed the envelope to Post-Office, Red Deer. The four of us piled into the democrat, and we were on our way to Notre Dame de Lourdes. That was the name of the small village with its post office and church, where we went to mass. This mission had been founded by French monks. Near the monastery and the model farm, there were a school and a rectory. As we approached the wooded hill on which the mission stood, we could see, arriving from the four cardinal points, the most motley assortment of vehicles I had ever set eyes upon: wagons with muddy wheels, shiny, varnished buggies, democrats, and all sorts of riders on horseback, from authentic-looking cowboys to bareback riders. However, everyone was well dressed and there was a "joie de vivre" that seemed to communicate itself from one person to another. The church was full, so that I could penetrate only a few feet into it and stood by a pillar. On it, I noticed bulletins of all sorts, as well as a list of parishioners who had or hadn't paid their dues. This struck me as a rather indiscreet discipline. While I was thus distracted, I felt a hand seize my arm. . . . It was Henri, who had come with the Boignots. What a joy to feel his closeness as we both smiled! In the meantime, the priest had gone up to the pulpit, and he was talking about the kindness of our Heavenly Father who takes care of each one of us. I couldn't help think about our own father out there somewhere, who at his age had left everything for the unknown . . . and for us. Henri, I am sure, was thinking the same thing.

As we left the church, people joined into groups that mixed joyfully. Henri and I found a spot where we could speak more privately. I saw a kind of compassion in his eyes as he said to me:

"Tell me, you aren't too unhappy at old Louis's are you? I've heard people say that he is the most backward and avaricious person in the district."

I burst out laughing and replied:

"Isn't that funny! Old Louis says the same thing about Père Boignot! No, no. Don't worry. I'm well fed, I'm given work that I can do, and I think that they are really very good people; . . . the only reproach I could make is that they are a bit negligent when it comes to cleanliness."

"Well, it's the same thing with me. The young couple is fine, but the old man and his son only wash on Sundays!"

"Maybe it's a custom they got from the Eskimos to fight the cold," I said.

Time was pressing and Henri added:

"The proof that the Boignots are good people is that they gave me fifty cents so that we could eat at the restaurant. Around three this afternoon, the young couple will pass through Notre Dame de Lourdes on their way back from visiting a relative, and they will pick me up. We'll talk to old Louis about getting you back."

The old man had already left, and it was Gaudias whom we met. He had run into another French Canadian from down east, whose farm wasn't too far from old Louis's. The fellow's name was Trudeau, and he assured me that he would drop me off on his way back. At the Notre Dame de Lourdes restaurant, we ate a good meal, served in shiny dishes on very clean table-cloths, for only twenty-five cents each!

The following week, haying having been interrupted because of rain, I was initiated to the handling of an axe. Gaudias, although only seventeen years old, was already a master of this art. From the very beginning, he gave me sound advice. The first was that one should get used to working both left-handed and right-handed because, in brush clearing, the axeman couldn't always choose the side to work from, especially in cutting branches. The same applied in the handling of the long cross-cut saw. I wasn't to push but to develop a rhythm as I pulled on it. I was also shown how to sharpen my axe and saw, how to split wood, and how to tie logs with a chain in order to drag them out of the bush with the horses. Before long, I could light a fire, even if the wood was damp, and load logs on the wagon so that they wouldn't fall off. Gaudias would say to me:

"The real work in the bush is in the winter, with sleighs. That's the best time. If a log is too heavy, you tip your sleigh right up against it, roll it on with the peavey, and, then, pull the whole thing upright by hitching a team with a chain to the side of the sleigh. Same thing for hauling. No more holes. Everything is frozen . . . rivers, lakes, sloughs. Your trail becomes like a railroad track, smooth and shiny."

The work I enjoyed least was stump pulling. The stumps had to be at least one year old before any attempt could be made to pull them out, even with the horses. This work seriously modified my poetic ideas on the picturesqueness of the forest . . . and I secretly hoped that father wouldn't choose a homestead with too much bush on it!

The following Sunday, Henri arrived at mass with good news. First, a long letter from father who acknowledged receiving ours. In Alberta, he had found a slightly rolling land with open prairies between clumps of trees and bushes, and he claimed that it was easy to clear. The original settlers he had spoken to had assured him that, after the first four or five years, which had been difficult, they were now satisfied with their lot. He had not found suitable land yet, because the closest available homesteads were situated fifty kilometres from established centres. The other interesting news was that the Boignots had decided to hire me so that I could be with Henri. The crop had to be harvested, and speed was essential. When we talked to old Louis about it, he was agreeable but asked that I stay on at least for one more week.

The following Saturday, old Louis gave me three dollars and loaded my baggage onto Adrien Boignot's democrat. Adrien, however, did not take me to the Boignots but, rather, to another farm he had bought, closer to the railroad tracks leading to Portage la Prairie, where he had had a new house built.

The quarter section where I woke up the next morning,

after having spent the night on a pile of shavings, was in a very beautiful location. It wasn't very far from the railroad and was almost totally under cultivation, except for a few bushes and sloughs. I couldn't attend church, which was now ten kilometres away, so I stayed with the young Mrs. Boignot and her baby. She was kind and patient as she questioned me about the old country. I helped her prepare the meal for the whole family, including Henri, who were to join us that evening. They were to bring hay for the horses in one wagon and the furniture for the new home in another.

It was a real joy for me to be reunited with Henri, but, early next morning, we were both hurrying behind the binder, which spat sheaves of oats ceaselessly. These we picked up and set up in stooks of eight sheaves each. At noon, we were far behind the binder, and endless rows of sheaves lay sprawled out all over the field, waiting to be picked up. After lunch, the women folk came out to lend a hand, and, by nightfall, we put up the last stook in the cut section of the field. I admit that, this time, every single muscle in my body was sore, . . . and Henri was no better off than I. The women had left early to prepare supper. When we had fed the stock and the cows had been milked, it was eleven o'clock at night. We didn't get to bed before midnight. I was so tired that I spent the whole night dreaming about a deluge of sheaves that fell all over me. I felt more tired in the morning than when I had gone to sleep. But, there was work to be done, so I gritted my teeth and kept going. We were apprentices in this new trade, and it just had to be pounded into us! We started again on the uncut portion, and, after a while, I welcomingly began to notice that the sun hid behind the clouds, . . . and, after young Jeannot brought us coffee, a new energy seemed to ooze throughout my body; . . . so the work went on for days and days. Henri and I had become as brown as natives, and our toughened hands didn't feel the bite of sharp straw or wild-rose stems. We both slept well and had the satisfaction of not being greenhorns anymore.

When Adrien's fields were all cut, we went to the Boignot farm, and there, too, when the binder had devoured I don't know how many balls of binder twine, we noticed all at once that the entire crop had been cut and stooked, . . . and we looked at each other in a kind of silly way . . . but not for long. These stooks had to be stacked for the threshing machine. The forks then came into play, and we hauled and set up stacks of sheaves in groups of four.

One day toward noon, Henri was on top of an almost-full rack of sheaves. He was standing at the back when the horses, bitten by horseflies, jerked ahead. Henri fell backward, trying in vain to grab onto a sheaf, and landed on his back from this twelve-foot fall. He turned slowly and moaned. I ran to him and tried to pick him up so he could stand, but he stopped me, saying that I was hurting him. I finally managed to have him kneel, but that was all; . . . I needed help. Adrien came, and the two of us tried to stand him up, but his legs wouldn't support him. The old man then arrived on the scene, and, remembering what I had heard about him, I instinctively extended my arm to protect Henri. Adrien seemed to understand.

"We'll have Henri lie on a cushion of sheaves and the old man will merely see if anything is broken."

Henri nodded and the old man, after having placed Henri on this temporary couch, went about his examination very gently. When he had finished, he said:

"My poor boy, you have displaced or bruised something in your back. You'll have to lie flat, without moving, for four days. Don't worry, it's not too serious. Are you suffering?"

"Not too much if I don't move," said Henri, "but I feel my legs won't support me; . . . maybe a few massages with camphorated oil might help me."

"We have some of that," replied Adrien.

We loaded Henri on a row of sheaves on a rack and slowly drove home. We placed him on a large sofa, and Adrien gave him a slow massage. The next day, his legs seemed to regain some strength. Two days later, he could stand with the help of chairs, but he could not walk. I was worried and suggested we might call the doctor.

"Monsieur le docteur," said old Boignot, "he must come from Treherne—that's twelve miles from here, . . . twenty-four miles return. When they sent him for Emile, we had to give him fifteen dollars, and he couldn't do anything. Have you the fifteen dollars? I haven't."

"We'll see tomorrow," Henri answered.

That night, I really prayed, and, the next day, my prayers were answered because Henri could take a few steps, but he couldn't straighten his back. He felt that eventually he would be fine and that Adrien should continue his massages. The sixth day, he walked slowly around the house with my help; . . . he had difficulty in sitting down and getting up again. On the following Sunday, we went to Notre Dame de Lourdes, and Adrien secured the help of a monk who knew something about medicine. He arrived and, upon examining the sore area, asked what first-aid treatment had been given. He then said:

"You've done the best. I believe that a vertebra has been displaced; . . . you'll have to avoid shocks and lie on your back as much as possible for a month before attempting any work."

Then he took me aside and said:

"You cannot leave Henri at the Boignots. Do you know anyone who could take him?"

I felt I was going to faint. How could I possibly know anyone except old Louis and the Boignots in this remote country! I consulted with Henri who told us that he had a friend named Domenech at the St. Boniface College. The monk knew Domenech and he decided.

"You'll stay at the monastery tonight. Tomorrow, a monk will drive you to Somerset. We shall send a telegram to Domenech so that he can have you picked up at the station in Winnipeg."

I think that I could have hugged that monk! Henri didn't seem perturbed at all.

"Marcel," said he, "run and tell Adrien to go back and fetch my luggage and to bring it here tonight, as well as the five dollars that his father owes me."

This was done, and, three days later, a neighbour returning from Notre Dame de Lourdes stopped by. He had a letter for me. Domenech had been happy to greet his friend; . . . the doctor had checked Henri and he was convalescing slowly. The college bursar had given him a job in the kitchen for as long as he required, where he could work in a sitting position.

Even if I was alone once more, I was happy with the turn of events. The Boignots, too, were satisfied and were very kind to me. The cutting was almost at an end when I received a letter from father, whom Henri had informed about his accident. He hadn't found what he was searching for yet, but a Métis guide was to take him into a new region. We were to be ready to join him as soon as he beckoned, because we had to be there in person to pick our homesteads and things had to be done in a hurry for fear of someone else taking the land before us.

The first sounds of the threshing machines far away toward Somerset reached us one evening, and a stranger came to our door to ask that we lend a hand to a threshing crew at a Belgian's home, whose wife was sick. The job I was given wasn't complicated. It consisted of filling, tying, and dragging the wheat sacks into the wagon box and standing them on end until the wagon was full. That night, Adrien went back and I stayed with the Belgian couple who were happy to know that I came from northern France, close to their country. The house was meticulously clean, and, late into the night, we talked about the old country . . . and the new one. The farmer's sick wife had even gotten out of bed to join in the conversation.

The next day, when I returned to the Boignots, who did I see getting off a democrat but Henri in person! He was thinner, pale, and slightly bent but walked with a cane. Henri had come with good tidings.

"I have received a letter from father, and we must leave immediately for Red Deer, Alberta, in order to register in person at the land office. The three of us are going to file for three-quarters of a section of land discovered by father and his guide Baptiste. The land is on the banks of the Red Deer River, sixty kilometres from the city. It's in the Stettler area mentioned to us in France by Father Guère."

Two days later, Adrien drove us to Treherne, which is situated on the main line of the CPR from Winnipeg to Calgary. We managed to find enough money for our tickets. We had about one and a half dollars left for the next two days. It was pretty close, but we had to manage.

IV

Home-coming on the homestead

The monotonous noise of the train wheels that had drummed in our ears from Montreal to Winnipeg began for us all over again. . . . We had to change trains twice in forty-four hours. Upon our arrival in Calgary, our meager rations were gone and we hadn't a penny left. Once again, we changed trains. Happily for us, the Calgary-Red Deer run took place at night and sleep appeased our stomachs. When we got off the train at Red Deer the next morning, father noticed that we weren't too frisky.

"Are you sick?" said he, almost before greeting us.

"Not precisely, but we are hungry," answered Henri with a rather sad smile.

"My poor boys! My poor boys!" was all that father managed to say as he emotionally hugged us both.

While devouring a substantial breakfast at the Chinaman's restaurant, we told father all about our Manitoba "odyssey." At nine-thirty we were lining up at the land office.

Father signalled to an elegant young man who was passing by. He stopped abruptly and came directly toward us. In a strongly German-accented French he said:

"Well, Mr. Durieux, I see that your children have arrived! So things are going well now! This morning, I saw the person in charge of homestead registration and yours are still free."

"That's excellent, Mr. Zimmerman. This is my son Henri, the eldest, and this is Marcel." Then, turning toward us father said, "Children, let me introduce my official interpreter in Red Deer. Mr. Zimmerman is from the Rhineland (here the interpreter winked at my father), and, at this time, he should be doing his military training in the area where I was a war prisoner of the Germans in 1871—at Coblentz."

"Ja! Ja! Mr. Durieux, . . . but if the Kaiser can do without me as well as I can without him, we should be good friends! But, Mr. Durieux, I seem to remember that you have another son who is presently doing his own military service, haven't you?"

"That's true. Mr. Zimmerman, you have a good memory!"

"Ja! Ja! Mr. Durieux. That is going to be good (and he lowered his voice and came closer) because your youngest one there, he isn't eighteen yet, is he?"

Upon hearing this, Henri turned white, . . . I blushed, . . . and father stared questioningly at the German.

"Therefore," replied Mr. Zimmerman, "as papers are not required, except for the immigration cards, we'll change the first name. What's the soldier's name? Jean? Fine! Give me the youngster's card, I'll take care of it."

In this way, three years before obtaining the definite title, at which time official proof of birth and age corresponding to Jean's age had to be presented, he would take my place, and I would have to wait one year before filing my own application.

Naturally, we were beginning to thank this kind interpreter (who was interpreting the law in his own way), but he stopped us with both his hands outstretched and said in a solemn tone of voice:

"My country did some harm to Mr. Durieux thirty-five years ago. I want to make up for it."

He then saluted us brusquely, with all his torso inclined before us, backed up two steps, and quietly walked away.

When our turn came at the office, Mr. Zimmerman was at my side. My father gave him the two other cards, and, as the forms were ready to be signed, the operation was completed in a minute, although I did hesitate slightly before signing Jean Durieux. After a lot of pleading, the interpreter consented to have lunch with us at the restaurant. He couldn't praise Frenchmen and, especially, French women enough. His dream, once his fortune was made, was to visit France, that beautiful country. I hope, for his sake, that his dream came true.

We left Red Deer early in the morning and, the following evening, arrived in Stettler without mishap. However, I must admit that there were some unexpected and frightening experiences along the way. If the main railroad lines of the country had settled with time, those between Lacombe and Stettler were only eighteen months old, and, according to the American Railroad Code, two frosts and two thaws were required before adding more ballast under the ties. We travelled for more than sixty kilometres on rails whose joints would sink four or five centimetres with each passage of a coach or box-car. This sinking caused the spikes to loosen gradually. Repeatedly, our train had to stop in the middle of nowhere as the whole crew walked in front and the conductor, armed with a long steel ruler, measured the distance between the rails. A kind of security council meeting was held out there in the wind; . . . and, at times, awesome-looking tools were taken from the tender. The boiler man, a kind of Hercules, used weights while the engineer pounded on the spikes.

Finally, with the speed of a hurrying snail, the locomotive attacked the danger zone; . . . the cars would slowly lean over, . . . and, just when we thought that they would topple, a happy jolt would right them once more. After a great deal of squeaking and grinding, we finally made it, to arrive in a concerto of bells and whistles (the locomotive bell, because there were no churches in Stettler at that time), one and one-half hours late.

The station we glanced at consisted of a cattle-car without wheels, placed by the side of a platform too short for our long, mixed train, so that, when we got off the coach, we found ourselves waist-high in prairie grass. I jumped first to help my father from the coach, while, with some difficulty, Henri moved our baggage. A man who was approaching shouted at us.

"Hello Mr. Durieux! Wait for me, I shall help you!"

It was a young and happy voice with the true accent of Brussels. The young man was wearing gold-rimmed glasses, his complexion was ruddy, and he had a blonde beard. He ran toward us, smiling while holding on to a pipe between his teeth. He noticed that Henri was having some difficulty with the suitcases and asked my father in a whisper:

"Is there something the matter with your tall son? Wait! Wait! I'm here to help!"

We were introduced properly while he was directing us toward a large cube-type of structure upon which a big sign read National Hotel. K. Stettler. Prop.

My father introduced this young man as a very good friend named Bonnevie, who had a business partner, a Swiss named Rossé . . . both were the owners of a general store. They had already helped father greatly, and Mr. Bonnevie was going to Europe, to Belgium, in six weeks. As mother and Jean were going to be at Soignies, fifty kilometres from Brussels, M. Bonnevie would see them at Christmas and they would make plans to travel back together at the end of March.

As we were entering the hotel lobby, we ran into a gentleman and Bonnevie exclaimed:

"What a surprise! Gentlemen, allow me to introduce Dr. Authenec. He's from Angoulême and, two years ago, settled between Ewing and Content. He came to Alberta in the hope of curing a nervous disease that at times causes a partial paralysis. Doctor, allow me to introduce the·Durieuxs, who have just gotten off the train. They've filed three homesteads fifty miles south on the Red Deer."

We shook hands with the doctor, who told us that he had heard about us through the Métis. The enterprising Bonnevie then said to the doctor:

"If you are not leaving right away, I wonder if you couldn't give the eldest Durieux, here, a medical examination. At first glance, he doesn't appear to me to be in shape to take on the hard life of a homesteader!" (I found out later that Bonnevie had had some medical training.)

We then went to shake hands with Bonnevie's associate, Mr. Rossé of Stettler Outfitters. He was a buoyant and jolly type, apparently afraid of nothing. As he had a good command of French, English, and German, he knew everyone within a radius of one hundred kilometres.

After this introduction, we proceeded to visit the town. It was barely a hamlet. Beyond a big empty space by Bonnevie's store stood the post office. Next was a general store owned by two Americans; across the street was situated a hardware and tinsmith shop belonging to a Scotsman, where all the tools, utensils, and equipment for settlers could be found. On the main street, which was at right angles, stood the National Hotel. By accident, we met the owner. He was a tall and jovial man, a compatriot of Rossé's who was from Chaux de Fonds (Switzerland), and papa Stettler was from Basle; . . . this explained why he spoke French hesitantly. He seized my father by the shoulders and laughingly said in a gruff voice:

"So! When are you going to lick the Prussians? Ach! Nasty people! Come on in, I'll buy you a drink, . . . but I must warn you, it won't be as good as in France."

Later, as we continued our tour, we found a lumber yard, a blacksmith shop, and a livery stable; then, a house that belonged to a Dr. Donovan (an Irishman who liked his liquor); and, finally, the Chinese restaurant and cleaners. On our way toward the station, we came upon a butcher shop and a bakery. We were soon back on main street where stood the Merchant's Bank and the National Bank.

All around us, beyond the village, an immense and virgin Nature spread before us. The land was slightly undulated. There were groves of willows, poplars, and birches through which we could see a large slough reflecting a small farm and straw piles like small dead volcanoes. I attracted my father's attention to them.

"You'll see. Our homestead way out there," said my father pointing toward the south, "you'll see; . . . it's quite something else!"

That night, in Dr. Authenec's room, there was a long consultation that I did not attend, but, when I saw the group coming down into the hotel lobby, I quickly understood that something was amiss.

"The doctor here finds it unsafe to take Henri with us into the wilderness; . . . his legs and back are too weak. He needs more rest. Since this is 8 October, it is best that we find a home for him in a more civilized part of the world than our first installation. Henri says that he could return to St. Boniface and to his job at the college there, where at least he will be assured of room and board. In the spring, the Bonnevie-Durieux group will pick him up on their return from Belgium. We shall miss Henri's help greatly, and it does mean another separation. However, complaining won't help matters much!"

A jovial voice was heard coming from the door of the lobby.

"Well! Well! Papa Durieux! Don't look so crestfallen. Is there something wrong?" It was the happy Rossé who, tapping on my father's back, continued, "Come now! We mustn't get upset. First, let's all go to the bar and have a drink. Nothing like it to set a head back in its proper place! And, after all, there isn't that much cause for the devil's funeral. Henri is going to return to Manitoba to build up his strength; . . . he's not the most unfortunate one. Isn't that right? In the meantime, with Baptiste and friend Boulot, you'll set up your camp and build your small home, and, after the winter, happy days again! Ah! Ah! When good mama Durieux arrives; that's what is missing! Patience, . . . patience! With the return of the sun, all of that will come: the Mrs., . . . your son, . . . and good old Bonnevie! There he comes now. Heh! Maurice! Come over here and console poor old papa Durieux who has got the blues."

That evening ended on a much more optimistic note. The next day, Henri stayed with us, and, toward evening, we went to the station to watch the train come in. We already looked at the newcomers with the protective air of twenty-four hour oldtimers.

Once Henri had left for Winnipeg, we had to prepare our own departure for the homestead.

"By the way," I asked, "what's the name of the place we are going to?"

"My friend," Rossé replied, "it hasn't got a name yet; you'll have to find one for it. For a time, your post office will be Stettler. That's it! One hundred kilometres return. There's a post office at Ewing, close to Dr. Authenec's. It is about half way to Stettler, but it's Mr. Ewing's farm where the mail is delivered every Saturday. There is no store there. As you have to continue coming to Stettler for your provisions and your construction materials, you may as well call for your mail here."

Bonnevie, who was watching the people go by in front of his store, suddenly exclaimed:

"There's Mr. Durieux with his dear Baptiste; only they don't seem to be in agreement."

"Isn't that the Métis guide?" I asked.

I saw a man who was a whole head taller than my father; he was slim and bow-legged in his high-heeled boots from which enormous spurs dangled. He wore tight-fitting trousers held up by a red-leather belt all studded with copper nails, which was criss-crossed by a cartridge belt. His jacket was of cloth and unbuttoned, and under it appeared a shirt with red and green squares. Around his neck was a many-coloured handkerchief that fell sideways upon his chest, and, finally, under a worn and flabby Stetson, a face appeared, ravaged by all sorts of scars. A long aquiline nose seemed to hover over a few greying hairs: an excuse for a mustache! His lips, to which a cigarette butt seemed to be glued, were thick. More striking, however, were two greenish, shifty eyes. Whenever you were lucky to catch those eyes, you had the impression that they were slightly amused at watching you. . . . Even his ears seemed to move. What a marvel! I forgot to listen to what Baptiste was saying in a slow drawl and that peculiar French of his.

He then pulled out a corn pipe, and, as Rossé had asked him an embarrassing question, he prolonged the cleaning of his pipe with his jackknife and with the gouging away at a tobacco plug of the same colour as his hands. He crushed the tobacco between his palms and ground it, filled his pipe methodically, and laboriously proceeded to light it! He then said:

"Well, listen my old Rossé, . . . let me tell you; . . . I understand old man Durieux here; . . . he payed me well, . . . but I helped him a lot too. . . . I found him good land. . . . No! No! Bonnevie, let me continue; . . . it's no joke!"

"I too understand," interrupted my father, "you don't want to come back with us because you are afraid of seeing Seymour and Freer, the two Englishmen established on the border of our half-section, who paid you to keep settlers away!" Baptiste was very uncomfortable. He lit his pipe again, shrugging his shoulders. "Yes, Baptiste, you said it yourself to Father Bazin of Trochu Valley; . . . you can't tell me that you didn't work with the surveyors and that you didn't happen upon the Englishmen's house, which was straddling the roadway and land reserved for homesteads? When, later, they found out that you were a guide for new settlers, they asked you not to prospect in that area, and they payed you well for it. It was easy enough for you because it's a dead end, caught between ravines and a high hill. You brought me there only in the end, Baptiste; that's why, when I visited them, you didn't want to come with me. . . . I had to make do with the little English I know, and, when I showed them on the plan what my land was going to be, Freer pointed to the emplacement of their house. I thought I understood that they were asking for a one year delay to move, and I accepted."

Baptiste muttered some embarrassed words, but we could not convince him to help us set up camp and build our house.

We still counted on the services of Brice Boulot, a Burgundian who had filed his homestead six months before us and who was part lumberman and carpenter. A few hours later, we crossed paths with Baptiste as he was getting ready to return to Content, a small hamlet on Tail Creek. The cayuse upon which Baptiste was seated was anxious to leave. In perfect control, Baptiste appeared glued to the saddle as his holstered rifle whipped around. Barely loosening the teeth riveted to his pipe, he said:

"I'm going to see an Englishman; a guy named Foot. I know him well. I'll tell him to get ready to help you on your house. He's a good carpenter. His post office is Ewing."

Then, raising his index finger to the brim of his hat, he disappeared like a flash.

My father had been able to rent a team of horses and a wagon for the whole autumn from a Mr. Miraud, a man from Berry (France) who had filed a homestead somewhere near the Battle River, north of Stettler, and who, after a difficult start, fell sick. The poor fellow had to be taken to a hospital at Red Deer. We had bought a tent, which we loaded on the wagon with Miraud's tent, our two wicker trunks, three folding camp-beds, two mattress sheathes for straw, a small tin stove with an oven to cook biscuits, kitchen utensils, smoked pork, canned goods, flour, yeast, an array of groceries—rice, beans, potatoes, a bag of oats—and a combination of woodcutter and carpenter tools. Another team and wagon were rented, upon which we loaded an assortment of two-by-fours, beams, and boards, as well as a barrel of assorted nails.

We were on our way at early dawn on 15 October, the days being frightfully short at this latitude. The weather, however, was relatively mild. For the first ten miles, things went well. The road was almost straight north-south. There were fences on either side. We could see high stubble beyond which plows drawn by four horses traced long brown furrows. The bushes, which were sparse as we left Stettler, were now, it seemed, thicker and taller. My father explained that these areas had been spared from prairie fires for a long time by the sloughs that bordered them. It was true that around this area there were more sloughs bordered by willows than usual, . . . and this was also the beginning of our troubles. Between these sloughs, the trail descended into hollows that became more and more spongy, and the deep tracks left by our wagon wheels quickly filled with water. As we clambered up the other side of these hollows, the ground would become hard again, and the wagons rolled on.

For the last one and a half miles, the trail had suddenly taken a south-east direction, and we had already bypassed other trails on both sides. My father was examining a map drawn by a Mr. Noullet, to see where we were to spend the night. Upon arriving on an open prairie, surrounded on three sides by poplar and birches opening in front upon a circular slough, my father raised his arm and signalled to stop. It was after one o'clock. The horses were tired and hungry and so were we. We unhitched the teams, led them to the water, and gave them a few oats while we tried to make tea. The other driver seemed accustomed to this sort of thing, and, before we knew it, he had prepared everything, including starting a fire from dead wood.

On our way from Stettler, so far, we had seen about ten farms, more or less removed from the road, but, after this halt, we must have travelled for two hours without sighting a cabin. The driver of the second wagon seemed worried, and I understood that he would have liked to meet someone to seek directions. Another hour went by. The sun was reddening the sky in the south-west, and the horses dragged on, tired. At each trail crossing, I felt that my father hesitated more and more. In fact, we had to admit that we were lost, because, having gone in a circle for half an hour, we found ourselves crossing our own trail.

We turned toward the south. Night was falling rapidly and the land seemed to rise. On the hillsides, our wagons threatened to roll over. We stopped on top of a hill. It was dark, and we were beginning to be completely demoralized. The other driver went out scouting and returned to tell us he had heard a cowbell, . . . but we couldn't figure out where the sound came from. We searched, and, in the end, I found myself alone, following the uncertain line of a bush, when I stumbled into a pole fence. I climbed through, and, suddenly, my feet were treading a freshly plowed field. I followed a furrow, and, as I reached a hilltop, my heart almost stopped beating. I had just seen a faint light close to the ground. It was too low to be a star, and the sky was covered with clouds. I left the field and fell upon a trail, which I followed. It passed between two sloughs. In front of me was a house, but there was no more light. I turned back, crossed the fence through a gate, and was fortunate enough to come upon our wagons. This, my father said, was not Noullet's place. What we did find in that big cabin built like an "isba" was a young Finnish couple and their two youngsters. The man, young, strong, and intelligent looking, did not know six words of English. He understood nothing of our questions, and the name Noullet left him completely cold. Finally, he came out of the house with a prehistoric lantern and led us to a clean barn where two oxen were peacefully eating. In an open stall, he spread three sheaves of straw and, inclining his cheek upon his hand, let us understand that these would be our quarters for the night. He then went out and began to unhitch our horses and showed us a small enclosure close to the barn into which he pitched many forks of hay. He then went back to our wagon and, pointing to the load, took on a questioning look, all the while bringing his hand to his mouth and pretending to chew vigorously. His mimicry was clear. I pulled out the pork, the biscuits, and the tea. With each article of food I removed, his face broadened into a smile, and he invited us into his house.

I've never regretted the bad luck that caused us to get lost that night, because never again was it given to me to admire such an interior. Imagine, for a minute, a rectangle made of tree trunks, superimposed and carefully made weatherproof with moss, . . . the whole thing roofed with split spruce logs covered with dirt! What was most striking in this cabin was the stove. It was made of dry clay, one and one-half metres high, two metres long, and as wide as it was long. In front, there were two doorless openings into which the logs were put. The smoke escaped by an enormous chimney of clay, occupying one-third of the end wall. The top of this rustic stove was flat and had a retaining edge. On top of it were placed rudimentary bedding, and two oblong wicker baskets tied by raw cowhide straps were hanging from the ceiling. I could imagine the two babies up there. A bench made of hewn spruce rested upon the side of the stove where I discovered a small oven closed by a tin door. In front, there was a rustic table whose legs had been sunk into the dirt floor, . . . and that was all! No trace of cupboards or pantry. Once the birch-lathed door, bricked with clay, was closed, I saw some sort of kitchen utensil that resembled a huge flower pot with black holes drilled at its base. Above it, a circular hole cut into the wall of the house served as a window, the pane consisting of an oiled bladder skin. In order to build this home, the owner had not spent a nickel.

We had brought in our kettle. The Finnish lady inspected it with curiosity. She understood its use, filled it with water taken from a wooden pail, pulled out red embers from the elevated oven, emptied them into the flower pot, and placed the kettle inside. At that moment, the owner came in with washed potatoes, which he spread upon the coals in one of the openings of the big stove. I went out to get a pot of jam, and all went so well that, in half an hour, we were all in a tight circle around the table where grilled pork, burning-hot potatoes, tea, soda biscuits, and jam were enjoyed by all . . . and where there were satisfied smiles and the nodding of heads in lieu of conversation.

After a good night's sleep on the straw in the barn, we went back to the house and proceeded to make coffee. We devoured a can of corned beef that seemed highly appreciated by the Finnish household, including the children, who had been let down from their baskets. What seemed to please them most was a handful of menthol candies that my father had bought to soothe a sore throat.

A high hill overlooked the Finnish homestead. We all climbed it together. On the left, between the hills that were covered with trees, about four kilometres away, a silver surface glittered in the sun. My father suddenly had an inspiration. Seizing the young man by the shoulders and showing him the shiny surface, he said:

"Lowden Lake?"

"Ya! Ya! Ya!" the man replied after a short hesitation.

"I see where we are now," said my father. "Noullet is about four miles from Lowden Lake toward the west. We've travelled too far east."

In fact, it was an English Canadian who set us back on

track as we reached his farm much later that day.

In spite of all the topographical descriptions we gave him, Mr. Noullet, a tall, bearded, and rather nervous man, never could piece together our nocturnal excursion. He had never even heard of the Finn who lived completely isolated from the community.

"I have an idea," he said. "Later on this afternoon, I shall travel on horseback with a bunch of fence poles and make a slash on each one. At each trail crossing, I'll plant the pole with the slash facing the direction you must take."

The plan was executed and, later, did save us from many a misadventure.

We had taken leave around eleven o'clock after a light meal. We feared that the second part of our journey might prove more difficult than the first—by now, we had no more illusions. After three miles of travelling, the countryside had changed completely. We were now entering a series of treeless hills whose summits were strewn with big, round stones. Here and there were small sloughs surrounded by willows and, on the southern side of them, by small shrubs with shiny leaves.

"Those are Saskatoon bushes," said father.

Later, I was to find out how good they tasted. Finally, between twin hills, a beautiful panorama slowly opened up before us.

"We've reached Big Valley. At one time this must have been a river three kilometres wide, at the end of the Glacial period. Now, it's nothing but a big creek. It seems swampy on the edges. There's a ford ahead, but it isn't too safe."

In fact, the ford did look threatening. Numerous undefined trails seemed to indicate that previous drivers had hesitated before they crossed here.

"Maybe we should double up on the teams," I suggested.

"I think so too," said father.

It wasn't the other driver's opinion. He assured us that his team was perfectly able to ford the creek and that, should we have any trouble, he would come back to give us a hand. So we proceeded.

What we had feared, happened. In the middle of the stream, the back wheels of the wagon, too heavy in the rear because of the overhang caused by the long boards, sank so deeply into the mud that every attempt by the horses to pull out the load only worsened the condition. It was up to us to intervene. We unhitched the horses and waded hip-deep into the ice-cold water in order to hook our team in front. We were able to pull ahead a foot or two, and that was that.

We had to return to our wagon and unload it completely. The empty wagon was then moved alongside the loaded one, and we proceeded to transfer one-quarter of the load and to hitch our horses with the others. The two teams barely pulled out the quarter load. We thought that it might be possible to haul out the last part of the load without moving the lumber.... Nothing doing! Once again, we had to transfer the load for a fourth trip.

Our own wagon load was still on the other side. Again, we had to proceed as before, ... in small loads, ... and crossed back and forth three times. When everything was finally transferred (except two prairie chickens I had shot along the way and which I forgot), we loaded the wagons as they had been previously. The driver hitched his horses.

"Giddyup!"

The horses started with a bolt. They must have thought the wagon had stuck. They gave such a jerk that only the two front wheels followed. The tongue had broken in two. The previous attempts must have weakened it.

Thus, after loading and unloading nine times, we had to do it again. Fortunately for us, for there was no help for miles around, among our carpenter's tools we found the proper drill. Once the wagon was repaired, we had to load the two-by-fours, the beams, and the boards, one by one, ... and, by this time, we knew each one individually.

When we moved again, the sun had already set and night had fallen as we reached the other plateau.

"Fortunately, there's only one trail now, and there are no more creeks to cross. We can roll along in the dark. I'd hoped to camp at home tonight. It will have to wait until tomorrow."

The driver from Stettler lit a tenth pipe and cried:

"Giddyup boys!"

The noise made by our wagons had been heard long before we reached the de Bailleux Ranch. The boys had a very fine ear for unaccustomed noises. We heard someone yelling.

"Yoo hoo!"

"Yoo hoo!" I answered as best I could.

"Is that you, Mr. Durieux?" asked someone with a very strong Béarnais accent.

"Yes, yes! It is we!"

"Well! You must have had some adventure to arrive at this hour!"

In front of us, we could see a lantern swaying at the end of someone's arm. After another descent and another climb, we finally arrived near the end of our memorable trip! While we were unhitching and feeding our horses, father went to help Hubert de Bailleux, who was already cooking other dishes to reinforce the menu.

"Let him be," said Joseph, sucking on a cigarette butt, "Hubert loves to cook, . . . and I hate it! So, you see, we get along fine!"

At the description of our varied adventures, the brothers were most sympathetic. We hadn't really thought about our personal appearance so long as we moved, but, now that we were being told about it, we did indeed notice the condition we were in. (Our friend Musy's words in Montreal came back to me. He wasn't far from wrong. "An impossible country! Abominable roads!") Yes, of course, but others had gone before us, . . . and the proof was right here—those brave de Bailleux brothers, for example, whose cordiality and warmth boosted our morale while Hubert's tasty cuisine filled our stomachs.

Their house was relatively large, and we were able to set up our folding beds. I could hear my father's voice in the distance, fading away as he was telling the de Bailleux brothers why Henri had not come along, . . . and I fell into an agitated sleep.

Hubert gently roused me at dawn.

"Ho! Ho! my little Marcel, . . . and how do we feel this morning?"

I opened one eye.

"My, my! You don't feel too good, do you?"

In truth, I was stiff everywhere. I had a hard time sitting up; however, I had to because a smiling Hubert was handing me a plate on which there was a hot cup of "café-au-lait" flanked by two rolls.

"I see that your father did not bring Baptiste. I'm not too surprised; . . . he's as lazy as a snake; . . . he much prefers to roam around and get well paid for it!"

"Perhaps," I answered, "but he spoke to us about a certain man named Foot who apparently could help us with the building of our house."

"Of course! We know that man Foot. He has a home-stead three miles from here. He may be a good carpenter, but he surely isn't a horseman, . . . and he's an awful farmer. What he loves best of all is a full glass of whisky."

When we were ready to leave, the two brothers threw Mexican saddles on two fine riding horses, put on chaps, and, vaulting into their saddles from the back of the horses, proceeded to flank us like scouts.

"We have stray cattle out there toward the valley. It's time we round them up."

When I saw those two fellows on their frisky horses, I understood why, a while ago, Hubert was so critical about the equestrian qualities of Mr. Foot. . . . They even seemed to ride better than Baptiste! In fact, Joseph had spent three years in the French dragoons, and Hubert had adapted the principles of French military riding schools to the Canadian Far West! They were both elegant and versatile, so much so, that I saw them roll a cigarette while their horses were trotting. . . . I was spell-bound.

As we left the ranch, the countryside became rather hilly, and we had to zig-zag quite a lot in order to climb up to a plateau belonging to a Mr. Harrington, a big rancher who owned over five hundred head of cattle. From a high spot, the de Bailleux brothers indicated checkpoints ahead. They seemed very flimsy to me, especially in this succession of rolling hills, all of which seemed alike and which resembled the frozen waves of an endless ocean covered with a fleece of dry, fine grass.

The de Bailleuxs scouted ahead for us. We saw them stop their horses half-way up a hillside that cut off the horizon at an angle. When we had joined them, Joseph said in a rather solemn voice:

"Now, you are practically home. When you cross that summit, you'll see all of your land. Isn't this a beautiful view, Mr. Durieux? I can see why this part of the country seduced you. I must confess that it is much prettier than our own place, . . . but it is a rather out-of-the-way place; . . . you won't see too many people, . . . especially in winter." He then added as a sort of encouragement: "It's true that you northern Frenchmen don't like to talk as much as we southerners, isn't it, Mr. Durieux? However, if I may, let me give you a bit of advice. Be very careful not to start a prairie fire, especially at this time, or you would have quite a few haystacks on your conscience. We have to leave you now. Our cattle must be roaming somewhere around our friend Brice's place."

"By the way, should you see Boulot, tell him we have arrived and expect him tonight or tomorrow," said my father.

"O.K." replied Hubert, spurring his horse. "Good luck and good health to you. When you come by, drop in for a bite to eat!"

Joseph, having caught up to his brother, whistled to us that all was well in that peculiar whistle call of the Ossau Valley in France.

No more trails now. The one we were leaving turned left. Baptiste had previously explained to my father, who was now telling me about it, that the trail, which eventually led back to Big Valley, makes a large loop before reaching the Red Deer River and reaches the river by a deep gorge named Tollman Creek.

"There is a ford there, about twenty kilometres from here. If you travel in the other direction, toward the south-west, at about the same distance, you'll find the small community of Trochu, founded by a grandson of the illustrious general of 1870, . . . also the Fathers of Tinchebray, a Norman order, under the direction of Father Bazin. They have a mission there. There's also another priest named Father Renut who, in theory, must minister to the Catholic colony right up to Stettler, but, in fact, it's difficult for him to show up in different homes more often than once every four months."

We were now rolling on a thick carpet of almost dry, fine grass that cushioned the soil completely. The blades, as fine as horses' manes, formed successive intertwined layers like a fleece, . . . produce of annual growths since the last . . . the last prairie fire! This was buffalo grass. It had fed those huge beasts for centuries, summer and winter. Even the wild horses, the ancestors of the cayuse (as Baptiste would say), fed on the same diet. In winter, they would paw the snow with their hooves and eat the dry grass and powdered snow, by which they ate and drank at the same time.

We continued climbing the high, long slope when my father exclaimed:

"Look over there! Those are the tracks we made three weeks ago, when I came with Baptiste. We can still see them!"

Our two horses seemed to understand and, ears pointed, turned as if by instinct into the tracks, following the trail that now imprinted itself well under the weight of our two wagons. This trail was to be well marked before snowfall, because it was the only way up that hill.

I was walking alongside the wagon and watching the wheels cut deep into the grass when I was interrupted.

"Marcel! Look!"

I froze in my tracks. Indeed, this was the promised land! My eyes filled with admiration. An immense, limitless panoramic view spread before us. The driver, who had joined us, nodded his head and exclaimed:

"By Jove! It's a nice place! I tell you boys, it's a nice place!"

V

The cruelty of the first winter

The gigantic trench of the Red Deer valley, one hundred and fifty metres deep and two and a half to three kilometres wide, opened at an angle on the right and curved majestically in front of us, to lose itself in a sinuous perspective far away on the horizon. On the left, a small valley surrounded by large banks formed an amphitheatre with almost regular steps up to the plateau. Completely overwhelmed by my imagination, I saw a sort of titanic coliseum with its flat racetrack on the bottom where a big, silver ribbon shone between the dark spruce. (I must state, however, to re-establish the proportions, that, when we reached bottom, the ribbon was one hundred and fifty metres wide!) Toward the south-east, at a great distance, a long, grey line cut off the horizon: the Hand Hills, sixty miles away. We were now on our land. As we continued descending, there was a gentle slope to the south-east. Father was already talking about unloading so that the driver could go back to Stettler. Once our camp was set up, we would also have to return for another load. As we reached bottom, I found myself gazing at cliffs covered with spruce thick as grass. On the more gentle slopes, bushes of poplars and birches were swaying in the wind.

The weather, fortunately, was beautiful. This allowed us to set up our stove on the grass. Following my father's indications, I found a small spring among the willows below a cliff. As I plunged the pail into the water, half-a-dozen red partridges took off in front of me (I remembered the two prairie chickens left on the banks of Big Valley). In the meantime, father was preparing the food, and, having set my pail down, I helped the driver unload the wagons. He had already given his horses a drink and a good portion of oats. He had a long way to drive. He hoped to reach the Noullet home that night and to be in Stettler the next day for lunch.

After he left, we set up our two tents in the shelter of the hill, which protected us from the north-west wind. In one tent, we placed our perishables and the two trunks; in the other, the camp-beds and a big wooden box that could be used as a table. We placed it by the stove whose pipe protruded through a tin rectangle in the tent ceiling. Finally, in a small bush sloping toward the spring, we constructed for the horses a rather temporary and rustic shelter of branches and ferns.

Night had fallen. Boulot, apparently, would not come. The lantern was lit and we prepared to bed down for our first night as "settlers."

The wind blew through the large, black hole of the deep valley, carrying along with it the noise of the river flowing on its gravel-bed. Stronger gusts would bring us its whisper as it reached the tops of the spruce on the other slope of the ravine. It seemed to me, however, that it carried other lugubrious noises . . . like a Tyrolean song. I questioned my father, who smiled and said very simply:

"Coyotes!"

I'll grant that this long howling complaint in the night did impress me. It seemed to me that the coyotes, too, were frightened, because I wasn't at ease, . . . and my hand instinctively sought the place where I had left Bonnevie's gun on the harness. My father, who had seen my gesture, got up on his knees and, lifting the opening of the tent, motioned to me to follow him.

We walked out for about fifty feet.

"Look at the reflection of the moon's crescent right over the elbow of the river."

Through the enormous crevasse, thirty metres away, I could see, far away and very deep, the glimmer of the crescent in the water.

"Now, turn around," said my father.

Through the tent walls, the reddish glow of the lantern seemed like a huge firefly. I heard my father say:

"Good Lord! How all this appears small in this immensity!"

I was trembling in spite of myself because the air was brisk.

"Let's go in, I'm cold."

"Yes," he replied, "we'll go to bed even though it's only seven o'clock."

Inside the tent, the stove had given off a certain amount of heat, which warmed me up and set my heart back in its place. In this fragile cloth rectangle, I had the impression of being in a citadel . . . and that the two of us could resist anything; . . . however, father thought that it might not be a bad idea to check the stakes and the tent ropes. . . .

My father had to shake me in order to wake me up from a very deep sleep. Coffee was made, and Hubert de Bailleux's rolls were here, by the Red Deer River! I ate heartily, went to let the horses out, and tied them to a post by means of long ropes so that they could graze at ease.

"As Boulot will be here today, you'll probably have to fetch some hay at Seymour's and Freer's."

"Do you mean to feed Boulot hay?" said I, without thinking.

My father laughed and replied:

"Of course not! But we need it to stuff those mattress covers. These camp-beds are as hard as boards!"

I was rather worried and embarrassed as I left with the wagon. I was shy and timid by nature, and I rather feared, like Baptiste, facing those two Englishmen, whose peace as first occupants of the area we were disturbing. What was to be my attitude as I introduced myself and at the same time requested help from them? What was theirs going to be? I had little choice. As I approached our neighbours' ranch, I heard the bawling of cattle. There were about thirty head. This loud noise forced me to overcome my shyness, and it was in a burst of laughter that the introductions were made. In a corral, the calves were bawling continuously. They had just been separated from their mothers with whom they had roamed since birth.

"Next week," said Seymour with a severe look, "we're going to brand them with a red-hot iron and that'll knock the bawling out of them!"

I made my request but had to repeat it over and over again because, by now, the cows had joined the chorus and the noise drowned out my hesitant voice and my rather "muddy" English.

In another corral, a stronger one, there was a real mountain of hay. I was given so much of it that I had difficulty climbing back upon the load. I was still very shy. I had been told in Manitoba that a young man like myself must never extend his hand first, and neither Englishman had shaken hands with me when I arrived. So, as shy people often do, I brusquely thanked them. It was then that Freer, in a rather sarcastic tone, asked me if I needed anything else. Naturally, I did what I shouldn't have done; . . . I took on a rather offended look and replied that we now had all we needed. Despite his big mustache, I did clearly see a semi-disdainful smile on Seymour's lips. For a greenhorn, I surely had made a fool of myself!

When Boulot arrived at lunch time, he raised a few complaints about his promise to help us. Baptiste had dropped us, now Boulot was threatening to do the same thing. Boulot finally made it clear that he needed a little more time to finish the work on the loft of his house. He wasn't going to spend the winter at his place, and he wanted to store some of his belongings up there. My father and he agreed that, the following week, he would give us two or three days.

The next morning, we tackled the foundations and the cellar. The soil, partly sandy, was easy to dig. After three days of work, everything was ready, and I left for Stettler to bring back a load of floor-boards, hoping to return at the same time as the other wagon that was supposed to wait for me. When I reached the Big Valley ford, I saw that some kind hands had placed branches and big logs in the bed of the small river, and I was able to cross it easily. I learned later that the de Bailleuxs were responsible for this friendly gesture. Between the valley and the Noullet home, I met the other load which had been sent by Rossé in the belief that we were already out of lumber. I made two trips, with a half load in each. Miraud's horses were not very strong, and, when I arrived, it was already pitch dark. I could see, however, that, during my absence, Boulot had returned and that he and my father had put up the studs and rafters.

A rather strong wind had arisen in the afternoon, and,

while I was having a bite to eat before bedding down, I heard what seemed to me to be a cracking sound. I went out to tighten the tent ropes and, glancing at the flimsy framework, reasoned that the wind couldn't possibly have much hold on that.

I was suddenly awakened by the loud flapping of the tent. The storm had unleashed completely. (I didn't even have time to think about Musy's prophecy in Montreal . . . that our house would be blown away like a match box!) A huge cracking noise, increasing in strength, suddenly ended with a huge bang as our tent was being raised by the air pressure. My father jumped out of his bed and we both rushed outside. We first noticed that half the other tent was flattened, squashed under an entanglement of studs and rafters, some of which were broken. Had our tent been closer, we would have received the whole thing on our heads! Some time later, the storm seemed to subside as if satisfied with its work, while, between the galloping clouds, the crescent of the moon ironically lit up the disaster. For our first try at construction work, we certainly had succeeded! We returned to bed, knowing full well that it wouldn't fall again.

The next morning we had to tackle the mess. Only the floor joists remained in place. About one-third of the two-by-fours were broken, and the other third were either ripped or split. When Boulot arrived, he joined the lamentations. Even after two hours of work, it seemed that we had done nothing, but, toward evening, we began to see what was usable.

While we were busy, a horseman pulled in. He was riding one of the de Bailleux horses, but the rider was unknown to us. He dismounted, greeted us very politely, and introduced himself as a cousin of our friends. He brought us news that Hubert had seen Foot, and that, if we needed him, he was prepared to come.

"We could surely use him," said my father.

The next evening our expert arrived. He was riding an old nag, which he held onto as if by some miracle. When he dismounted and saw the mess we were in, he smiled, nodded his head, pulled out a small pipe, a jacknife, and a plug of tobacco, and proceeded to do as Baptiste had done! He almost used the same language.

"Well, boys! I'm going to tell you something. . . ."

We had no doubts as to what he was going to say, . . .

and we didn't expect compliments and congratulations. He was so comical in his clownish way that we couldn't help but forgive him. He saw that I couldn't help laughing and drily said:

"Say, Frenchie! I believe that you are laughing at me, aren't you?"

"No! No! I laugh for not to cry!" I replied in my broken English.

"Well, then, let's take a look at what's missing. I'll measure what's spoiled."

The next afternoon, I was on my way to Stettler, with a stop-over at Noullet's, to bring back a load of lumber. Two days later when I returned, there stood a building without doors or windows yet but able to resist a strong wind. Foot worked well and fast, but father had to give him a good shot of whisky after each meal to get him going.

I found myself learning to handle a hammer and helping lay on the shingles. Somehow, deep inside, I felt that the building of this home constituted some momentous episode in this part of Alberta; . . . I was day-dreaming when Foot interrupted me.

"Marshall [that's how he pronounced my name], your dad, there, is a nice and fair old gentleman, but he has damned foolish ideas as to how to build a house with lumber. I, too, come from the old country, and I know damn well that this isn't how we build out of lumber. The old gentleman made me put a row of felt paper under the clapboards outside, but the paper isn't joined. There's nothing on one side to hold it against the studs. Same thing inside. When the blizzards blow this winter, you're going to hear that slack paper flop around in there, and then the wind will come through. That's certain, Marshall! However, I did as I was told!"

Smoke was now rising through the stove-pipe. The wind was getting colder, and the hammers hurriedly pounded in the last nails. As he came down the ladder, Foot announced that he was going to leave the next day because he had to haul firewood for the winter.

"By the way, Marshall, I don't see any wood pile. You're going to be caught by winter, . . . you'll see! Next week, I shall come and adjust the doors and windows."

As I climbed down the ladder, I thought I heard the noise of harness chains as they slacken on the traces when a team comes down a hill. Those visitors must be for us. In the last light of the setting sun, I could distinguish six heads in a very large type of democrat. A voice was guiding the horses.

"That," said Foot, "is the voice of Xavier, Baptiste's cousin. He must be showing land prospectors some of the country. Hello, Xavier, old man, what the deuce brings you here tonight?"

As Xavier spoke French Métis, my father went out to greet him. Xavier tried his best to be polite.

"Well, you see, those people, they come from the States. They're looking for a place, so I brought them down here. Don't disturb yourself for us. We have a big tent and all we need for the camp. We would appreciate firewood and water."

When we had eaten, I went out to take a look at Xavier's camp. He certainly had a big tent. Some parts of it had been repaired by old flour sacks, probably by his wife. What appeared strong were the posts and stakes. Upon my return, Foot made the following remark:

"If the wind ever gets stronger, I'm afraid Xavier's outfit is going to be blown away; the ropes and the main part of the canvas are rotten."

It was true that the walls were thin. As we looked at it in the dark, we could clearly see the shadows of the occupants as they passed in front of the lantern.

We were surprised by an unexpected visitor whose swinging walk I recognized as that of Boulot.

"Good evening, everyone! Can you put me up for the night, Mr. Durieux? I've decided to spend the winter in Red Deer, and it was too late to go to the de Bailleux ranch . . . so I took it upon myself to ask for your hospitality. I've had my dinner, thank you; tomorrow, I'll go to Ewing with the de Bailleuxs, and from there to Stettler with the mail courier."

"That's fine, Boulot, only you'll have to sleep on a mattress. We have a visitor, Clérisse, the de Bailleuxs' cousin. Tomorrow, I'll give you two letters to mail."

We sat around our own table for the first time. Foot had built it in one hour. For our feast, there were two prairie chickens killed by Clérisse, fried potatoes, and a cake. Outside, the wind seemed to be shifting. I went out to get more wood for the following morning; . . . the new-model stove literally devoured the stuff. It's true that our stove-pipe was much longer now. Already, Xavier's tent was pretty shaky in the wind.

The five of us bedded down as best we could for the night, amongst our baggage, equipment, provisions, etc. There was very little room left. I was lying in the north-west corner of the house, from which direction the wind was coming, and, by now, it was howling. My head lay close to the wall. The coal-oil lamp was put out, and, soon, I could hear Boulot's snore, . . . but another noise much more powerful came from outside. There was a storm brewing, and it came directly down from the north. My ear, close to the boards, could perceive what Foot had predicted, . . . the felt paper inside was flapping around! I could feel icy air coming through the joint. I covered my head so as not to catch cold but couldn't sleep. The storm now seemed to be in full swing. I couldn't resist looking outside. By sitting up in bed, I could see through the window.

I noticed that the lantern was lit in Xavier's tent and that the tent was undulating. I recognized Xavier's silhouette outside as he tried to consolidate the tent. Our house was creaking under the wind. Suddenly, I saw the tent being torn in half and one side of it blow out like a sail. It resisted for awhile and, then, took off into the wind.

I awakened Foot, who was sleeping on a pile of shavings. As he was already dressed, we lit our lantern and rushed out into the squall. Xavier's lantern guided us. All the men were there, but the horses had disappeared. We managed to recover the blankets and provisions and, skidding back toward the house in the snow, we all piled in. We were now eleven! The house's solidity reassured us, but our problem was to find room to sleep.

In the meantime, my father prepared tea. One of the Americans pulled out two flasks of whisky from his jacket, so that a second housewarming was held. We tried to organize some sort of sleeping plan. Foot and Xavier had pulled the two benches together and, half seated, half reclining, continued to speak in a low voice. Without moving from his place, the Englishman kept mechanically putting wood on the fire, while Xavier, who had just inherited a new plug of tobacco from one of his customers, had taken on the task of carbonizing as much as he could before morning. Those two characters never seemed to get tired! Foot had somehow managed to lay his hands on one of the flasks and kept pouring some of its contents into his tea. I seemed to be floating and kept dozing off and awakening. Foot's monotonous voice droned on and on, . . . and Xavier patiently absorbed this flow of words and seemed to approve by nodding his head and once in a while repeating Huh! Huh! The storm kept on roaring outside; . . . I finally fell asleep.

A big lamp that had been lit awakened me. The smell of heated lard hit my nostrils. Foot and Xavier were making pancakes. Two Americans, straddling the benches, were munching away. Those pancakes must have been pretty tough because the dough had neither eggs nor milk! I noticed the alarm clock . . . a quarter to four, . . . and daylight wouldn't be upon us until eight-thirty.

In the morning, Xavier climbed up the hill and began to emit some sort of eerie call. Five minutes later, the two cayuse, dry-haired and round-bellied, appeared. They had spent the night in a sheltered gulley. Once the horses were hitched and the democrat reloaded, they all left, with Boulot as an extra passenger. That night, Clérisse and I left for the de Bailleuxs with Miraud's team. He required them in Stettler. I had to journey the whole way back on foot. I arrived rather tired, but we did have two comforting letters: one from France and one from St. Boniface.

As we kept on heating the house, the interior boards began to shrink, until a small finger could be inserted between the cracks. We probably could have nailed laths over the openings, but we had run out of lumber and had no means of transportation. I had reminded the de Bailleuxs to bring us the quarter of beef as soon as they had butchered and, also, a can for coal oil, ours having sprung a leak when the house frame fell on it. Two days went by without any visitors.

During the night, I awoke and noticed a faint glow on the ceiling. It came from the windows, which had no curtains or shutters. By gluing my eyes to the window-pane, I saw millions of little white particles . . . snow! On the ledge, three inches had already piled up. At nine o'clock, the sky was barely clear and the snow kept on falling. I couldn't see more than ten metres in front of me, as the wind was blowing the stuff diagonally across. It was twelve degrees below zero. In the afternoon, I went down toward the creek to fetch wood, but it was all covered! Wouldn't this ever stop?

It did, but only the following afternoon when the snow was thirty centimetres thick. That night, the temperature went down to minus eighteen, and the following morning it was minus twenty-two. The pail, which had been full of water and had remained by the door, was completely frozen. The pickle jar had burst, and the ink in the bottle had been transformed into black marble.

As there had been little or no wind, the snow was just about even everywhere, except at the spring, which never froze. Two days later, it was quite something else . . . a blizzard! The storm was as violent as the one that had carried away Xavier's tent, only this time it carried with it billions of very fine and sharp snow granules that literally burnt my face! In two hours, the snowbank on the north-western corner of the house was a metre high, and the wind, continuing to form dunes, blew the snow off this bank right over the top of the house. On the other side, another snowbank was forming; longer and rounder, it ended up looking like a long, white, grounded whale.

Naturally, I spent more than half my time searching for dead wood in the ravine by the spring. Each day, I had to go farther and farther afield. Our big worry, however, was that we had left only two cans of corned beef, two cans of salmon, and a piece of cheese.

The temperature that night dropped to twenty-nine below. I awoke from my sleep to feel the sharp pain of frost-bite on my cheeks, nose, and one ear. I got up rather worried. My father, who could not have been sleeping, heard me. We looked at each other for a moment and read panic in each other's eyes. Our blankets were covered with frost, and, as for the windows, we had to use a knife and scrape away at them to find the pane. Dad lit the fire and we thawed out the kettle and made tea, a very sweet tea, to which we added a spoonful of whisky. I felt better, especially after those few seconds of fear. We had to avoid discouragement at all costs, or we were lost! The fire was kept alive, and, in the morning, I was back searching for wood. At noon, we opened the first corned-beef can and, in the afternoon, while searching for something in the trunks, I found, in the celluloid collar box, two chocolate bars from France. . . . Chocolate from France! For five months, I hadn't tasted any. My first impulse was to bite into a bar, but, on second thought, I thought it best to put them away.

One morning, the sky was as blue as the postcards from "La Côte d'Azur!" A bright sun rose above the horizon. Half an hour later, the frost on the exposed windows started to melt. By eleven, it was warm enough for us to open the door. It seemed that spring had arrived. Yet, this couldn't be spring; ... it was December. In the sun, the thermometer showed six degrees above zero. However, in the shade behind the house, the true temperature still read eighteen below.

The next day, there was the same kind of sunrise.

"Do you think that you could walk over to the de Bailleuxs today?" asked father. "We might have mail and I've four letters to post. You could tell them how low we are on food and come back with a fair-sized piece of meat. We shall also need coal oil."

How true! For the last ten days, we had been going to bed at night-fall in order to save our last candles.

As the crow flies, there must have been ten kilometres between us and the de Bailleuxs. Because of having to circle snowbanks, I should allow for one-half more of that distance. There were six and a half hours of daylight. Allowing for a little more than three kilometres per hour, I calculated that I could make it ... perhaps ... and come back the next day.

"I'll try," I said.

My experience in snow, until now, was limited to walking around the creek in search of firewood. There were a lot of bushes there; ... but, when, with my pockets loaded with biscuits and a bar of chocolate, I began to climb toward the plateau above the house, I saw that it wouldn't be easy. All the depressions were filled, and I sometimes found myself in snow up to my waist. Higher up, it was hard on top of the snowbanks, so I followed their crests, but, again and again, my weight would be too heavy and I would sink and have to struggle out. I found that I had to angle my way up and walk four hundred steps to advance forty.

Courage old boy, I said to myself, over the top crest, on the plateau, things may be better. From up there, one can see for twelve miles, and there might be a trail or an animal track.

In spite of the cold, I was hot and out of breath. I stopped to rest and unbuttoned my jacket. I had to take off my mitts, which were tied around my neck by a string. When I had rested, I buttoned my coat, pulled my woollen cap way down over my ears, put on my mitts, and tackled the last part of the slope. The air was so cold and dry that I could hear something like a long continuous squeaking sound in the snow . . . and a voice far off saying, "Steady now." Some driver was up there somewhere. I could hear the harness chains, but I was still far from the top. After a whole lot of sliding and tumbling, I finally made it. There was nobody in sight.

From up there, I could see the Hand Hills, much larger, they seemed, and much closer; . . . but, when I looked at the series of hills that led to Harrington's plateau and saw the height of the sun in the sky, I concluded that darkness would overcome me in this most thankless corner of the earth, where a poor soul could get lost in broad daylight . . . even without snow! I had travelled one and a half kilometres, and I had four hours left for eleven more. There would be no moon. It would be dark at four . . . and, at best, I would still be five kilometres away from the de Bailleuxs' home. I would probably freeze out there, and, without help, my father in a few days would too.

I had to think. The first advice I got was from my stomach. I needed strength. Once the biscuits and chocolate were down, in lieu of water I sucked upon an icicle gathered from a small branch.

"Now, let's see," I said. "I came this far to seek help. I can't go back empty-handed. The closest spot to my present position is the Freer and Seymour place [the two Englishmen who we had more or less forced to leave]."

In my mind, I could see the rather cold reception that awaited me after my behaviour the last time. The greeting would surely be . . . icy . . . this time.

"Beggars can't be choosers! I'll have to humiliate myself and acknowledge that I was wrong."

I walked on until I stumbled on sleigh tracks in the snow. These tracks must have been made by the Englishmen hauling hay for their cattle. I was now walking along the windswept crest, and snow only came up to my ankles, so that, before long, I arrived at the slope leading to the Seymour-Freer ranch. One more snowbank, one more climb, and I noticed a haystack about six hundred metres away, as well as two silver and parallel lines in the snow. I could distinguish tufts of hay on each side, a sign that the tracks were fairly recent.

When I stumbled into the Englishmen's shack, I must

have been quite a sight. Freer, who was alone, let out a gasp and his grey-blue eyes almost popped upon seeing me. He explained, as if in one breath:

"Good gracious! We thought you were both dead from the cold. We were just going to go down there to check on both of you."

"Well, we're still alive, but we have no more meat, no more coal oil, no mail, and we're having a hard time finding fuel."

Before I was through speaking, Freer had grabbed a frying pan in which a huge beef-steak rested in its sauce. He added two large spoonfuls of fried potatoes and put the whole thing on the red-hot stove.

"Why didn't you come sooner? And how is the old gentleman? As far as the mail is concerned, just wait a while. Douglas has gone to the Harringtons' who must have received it yesterday, Saturday."

"Is it Sunday today?"

"Yes, it is. Would you like more tea? More sugar?"

The real sympathy that I could read in Freer's eyes really embarrassed me.

Time passed quickly until Seymour's return, and, when later he came in and learned of our distress, I saw the same expression of compassion. He smiled and his big icicled mustache moved as he said:

"I've got the mail, and there are two letters from France and one from Manitoba."

I remembered my father's two letters and placed them in the metal box reserved for the mail and its next trip to the Harringtons'. Night was fast approaching, and I had to think about my trip back. I stood to dress.

"Wait a minute," said Seymour, grabbing a saw and an axe.

Freer, in the meantime, had found a small coal-oil can and proceeded to fill it from the large one. His associate returned with a huge cube of meat that he wrapped up in a flour sack and tied to my back. Then, putting on his big sheepskin coat and his greased moccasins, my new, bearded friend took a long stick from behind the door, picked up the oil can in his other hand, and said:

"I'm coming with you. I'll break the trail ahead. That should help."

That kind man accompanied me up to the bank of the creek that I had followed many times in search of wood. To get down the gulley, I let myself slide on my back, but, before I reached bottom, the meat pack flew over to the side and pulled me along so that I ended up rolling down the hill, meat pack, oil can, and all! When I finally looked up, I could see in the sunset the happy and childish laugh on Freer's face. He raised his long stick and cried out:

"So long! Come again if you need anything."

I arrived home as darkness was falling, to be greeted by a very surprised but happy father.

"It's only me! Look at what Freer and Seymour gave me."

When he had seen what I was bringing, father remarked:

"They should have damned us, and they are saving our lives!"

I then proceeded to describe for him my first adventure in the prairie snow.

That beneficial help allowed us to examine our situation a little more optimistically. The following week, the weather was calm and sunny. From the inside of the house, I heard the de Bailleux whistle (he alone could somehow do this through his fingers). We rushed out in time to see the two brothers, wearing long skis, as they came down the big hill. Upon seeing us, they stopped and waved their poles. Hubert yelled:

"We're bringing you steaks and light!"

In fact, we saw that they were drawing some kind of a sled loaded with a big, white bundle. They walked apart, each pulling from his own side. Suddenly, they flexed their knees, and, like the wind, they slid down the slope onto the plateau. They even went beyond the house and had to back-track. I couldn't believe it! When I thought of my own trip on foot and saw this, I was just amazed! My father, in the meantime, was saying:

"Well, well! That beats me! It's getting harder to believe each day! Where in the world did you ever learn to travel in this manner?"

"My dear Mr. Durieux, ten days ago I had never set eyes on a pair of skis in my life," explained Hubert, anxiously rolling a cigarette; and, while we were storing the rice, the beans, the beef, and a large coal-oil can full of coal oil, I heard him add: "Ten days ago, while Joseph and I were struggling in a snowbank, a fellow named Peterson, a Norwegian neighbour, whizzed by us on these long, wooden skates at the speed of a trotting horse. Well, said I to myself, old Hubert, that's just what you need to carry food over to the Durieuxs. We heard that he was making another pair for his wife. We went over to see him, and he loaned us the four skis. We practised for four days at drawing the toboggan, loading it more and more each day; . . . it's that simple. Say, Joseph, how much time did it take us?"

"Well, it must have taken . . . let's see. . . . We left at 10:30 and it's now 1:45. A little more than three hours . . . and, because we had some detours, we must have travelled eighteen kilometres. That's not too bad for beginners, especially considering that we were dragging about one hundred and twenty pounds."

A good coffee was prepared with biscuits and jam and a shot of whisky. Joseph got up to go first.

"We've got to put those things on again. We'll leave the toboggan for Marcel. He can make use of it to haul his wood."

When we saw the de Bailleuxs later, they told us that they had returned in less than two hours.

We were now safe, once again, as far as food was concerned. Our main problem was always that of fuel, . . . and we were now in the second week of December. It was getting colder each day. As we kept a fire going for only twelve hours, there was frost in all the cracks of the house. Our wood supply did not allow us to heat the house all night.

Two weeks before Christmas, I had found a new bush in a small ravine entrance up from the creek. I was fortunate enough to stumble on a clump of willows that had dried standing. The wood gave off a better heat and lasted much longer than poplar or birch. While I was working and had straightened out to rest my back, I faced the north-west wind coming down from the big crest above. My attention was attracted immediately to some kind of apocalyptic chariot that, half-way down the hill, was approaching rapidly. After my first surprise, I understood what it was. There came the front half of a bob-sleigh hitched to four horses, two heavy ones in the back and two lighter ones in front. All of this bounded up and down in the snow like dolphins in the sea. The sixteen hooves of these hairy and shaggy beasts raised such a cloud of snow that it fell on their backs and on the passengers I could imagine somewhere behind. The wind, blowing from above, caused this snow cloud to follow horses, passengers, and carrier down the slope. If a horse sank from time to time, the momentum of the others would pull him out. In spite of a thirty-below-zero temperature, the horses steamed like boilers. From time to time, I could see two heads emerging from a large, white box attached to the sleigh bunk. Soon, I was seen, and an arm kept waving at me. It wasn't the de Bailleuxs. I would have recognized the horses. Just then, this fantastic crew disappeared in a depression where the snowbank was so bad. As they were not reappearing, I feared that they might have gotten stuck and hurried as best I could to lend them a hand. But, I was wrong. The horses, whose nostrils were loaded with huge icicles, appeared, and I saw that their drivers had paused to invert the order of the teams and were proceeding to hitch the heavy horses in front. It made sense, since the trail ahead was really hard to break.

A well-known voice shouted to me.

"Hello Marcel! It's me, your brother . . . Henri. . . !"

Needless to say, I was surprised.

"Henri! Where in the world do you come from?"

"From Ewing Post Office. Jump on the runner at the back; . . . we'll have time to talk at home!"

I'll let you guess my father's surprise and joy.

Henri explained to us that a terrible epidemic of typhoid fever had broken out in St. Boniface and that the rapid spread of the disease had forced the fathers to close the college and send students and staff home for an indefinite holiday.

"I knew that the mail left Stettler on Saturday morning for Ewing and planned things so that I could catch a ride with the mail cutter, . . . except that we couldn't arrive at Ewing that day but today, Sunday.

"But, isn't today Monday?" asked my father.

(Somehow, we had jumped a day. After 31 December it was much worse because we had no calendar.) Henri continued:

"Once at the post office, I let it be known to the settlers who had come for their mail that I was looking for a way to reach my father's place, six miles south of the de Bailleux ranch. After a few trials, which didn't bring any results, this young man here came up to me and offered to help." As he spoke, he turned to the person in question and said in English, "I'm telling my father that you are a daring fellow!"

The young driver simply smiled and shrugged his shoulders as if to say that all this was really nothing. Henri continued:

"He then took me to his home where we ate a hearty meal, hitched up the four horses here to the forward bunk of the sleigh, and we easily reached the de Bailleuxs'. From then on, I often thought that we would have to turn back. . . . Anyway, we're here!"

Henri then opened an enormous package. He pulled out an assortment of canned goods and biscuits and, finally, a beautiful pipe, a gift from the college bursar, as well as a pound of American tobacco.

"This is for you," he said to the driver, who came from North Dakota and whose name was Steve Perkinson.

"I hear that there are a lot of mosquitoes in North Dakota."

"There sure are," replied Steve. "They're a real menace!"

"Over here," said Henri, "there aren't quite as many . . . especially today!"

This remark touched off hearty laughter on the part of Perkinson. Henri gave him the pipe, the tobacco, and a whole lot of biscuits, and, soon, this brave lad was on his way with his four horses, who would have an easier time of it now that the trail was broken.

In the years that followed, we met Perkinson two or three times. He always greeted us with a malicious grin and said in his own characteristic way:

"Not many mosquitoes today, are there?"

VI

Mother's arrival and the first mass

The unexpected arrival of Henri complicated our food problem. We needed some supplement to our diet. We knew, however, that, should we run short, we could always count on Freer and Seymour. In the meantime, I made it a habit of never leaving the house without the gun, because, when I did, I was sure to see game within shooting range. Henri, who was accustomed to sleeping in well-heated rooms, did not sleep too well the first night. The transition was rather brutal for him. When, in the morning, he saw the frost on the walls, he exclaimed:

"No wonder I was cold!" Having dressed, and putting the back of his hand against the crack on the wall, he added, "That's it! The wind blows through here. We'll have to keep the fire burning all night."

"Precisely!" I replied, "except that we have a fuel problem."

"Maybe we could stick paper all around," he suggested.

We tried, but half the paper ribbons did not stick. The hot and cold contrast cracked them as well. We continued filling the larger crevices with old pieces of cloth.

After a few days of prospecting together for wood, Henri had to conclude that we were fast approaching a crisis. That night, a council was held around the table, . . . and father remembered something that Baptiste had shown him in the cliff above the creek. He had seen a coal vein showing through up there.

"It's somewhere on the side of the cliff behind the

house. It's very steep, although there is a sort of round ledge that rises to the top at an angle from that spot. It faces the valley, toward the Red Deer. If one were to slip, there would be nothing to hold on to. With the snow, it would be dangerous. It's about sixty metres lower than us."

"Do you think we could get at it from the creek bottom?" I asked.

"It's impossible. There are two wall-like crags, and we would have to travel over one kilometre in the ravine. Tomorrow morning, we'll go and investigate."

Snow was falling the next morning, but there was no wind. We picked up our shovels, pick, and crowbar and were on our way. First, we had to cross the huge snowbank that was now over two metres high. Then, once on the slope, we angled up on half-frozen snow into which we dug steps down to the clay. Our work went on heartily. One of us used the pick while the other cleared the snow and ice. We weren't too comfortable working; one false move and we risked tumbling down one hundred and fifty feet . . . without hope of being rescued. At one o'clock, as we returned to the house for lunch, we noticed that our trench in the snowbank was half filled, yet, up along the edge of the cliff, there wasn't a breath of air.

The afternoon was a busy one, but at half past three the narrow corridor in which we were working was too dark to risk going on. We were, however, close to the small rise my father had spoken about. It took us two days of hard work to reach it. The weather held, and, after two hours spent clearing the topsoil, we saw the first signs of coal in the greyish-blue clay. At first, it was nothing but a mixture of clay and black granules, but, as we dug deeper into the frozen wall of the cliff, the coal became blacker and less easy to break. Finally, toward evening, we had extracted half a pail of lignite that was a little breakable but, still, with nuggets the size of eggs. As I climbed down at nightfall a terrible doubt entered my mind, and I said:

"What if this turns out to be nothing but a black stone. . . . or some sort of schist?"

"I surely hope not; . . . anyway, we'll soon find out," Henri replied.

When we had thrown two shovels full on the red-hot embers and replaced the lid on the stove, the three of us, I am sure, held our breath.

64 •

"That's it!"

The whistle of the liberated gas could be heard as the coals caught fire, and an unusual warmth spread toward our cheeks. What a joy! We could now see the metal itself taking on a cherry-red glow. My father joined his hands and said out loud:

"Thank you Lord for having had mercy on us!"

We then removed the lid to watch, and, like barbarians in front of something marvellous, our eyes round with admiration, we stared at the small mass, white with heat, which gave a comforting heat and warmed us completely.

With new hope, we got to the mine early, because, this time, there was no snow to shovel in our stairway. By the end of the afternoon, we had removed a thick layer of grey clay and the first layer of breakable coal, until we finally encountered the core lignite, hard and shiny, from which, by carefully working, we were able to extract chunks as big as two fists. When father saw the results of our efforts, his face lit up and he exclaimed:

"With that, we're going to be able to keep the fire going part of the night! We'll need about three pails a day. It's going to call for a lot of effort, especially the climb each time. We can only carry half a pail at a time; . . . that's twelve trips a day and there are 474 steps up there each time and two slopes. Counting ten pauses or so, it means one and a half hours per load. There's work there for a man all day long, . . . and that's without a blizzard!"

Around ten o'clock that night, the thermometer indicated forty degrees below zero. We piled all our clothes on top of our beds and covered our heads. I was awakened by the scraping of the shovel in the coal pail . . . and was surprised not to feel the cold. The lamp was lit, and father was filling the stove. He noticed we were awake.

"Boys," he said cheerfully, "we're saved! It's two in the morning. We loaded the stove at ten. I found a lot of glowing coals and was able to start the fire without using wood. We'll now have heat until seven this morning!"

What a satisfaction in the morning not to see frost on our blankets. There was hot water in the kettle and flowing vinegar for our bean salad. Beans were often on our menu, as well as rice, and, as a substitute for oil, we used lard. Milk, butter, eggs, green vegetables, fresh fruit, and potatoes we would not be able to taste before the end of March or the beginning of April. However, we had hopes now of not dying of cold and inanition.

With hard and tedious work, we were able to build up a coal reserve, which we stored in our cellar. The mine, however, had to be propped up, and for this we used green poplar poles, of which we had plenty. The whole thing lasted until the spring thaw, at which time the mine was abandoned.

Christmas Day and New Year's Day went by almost unnoticed. We used our old calendar and went back to January, allowing for the changes in dates and days of the week, . . . but we were not too sure of being right. In early January, the weather turned so cold that, even today, I tremble when I think of what would have happened to us had we not discovered the mine. For fourteen days and thirteen nights, the blizzard roared, whistled, and swept away without letup. It shifted from northwest to north to north-east, building up the snowbank on the north side of the house until it was over two metres high. In spite of the stove that glowed day and night, lumps of frost gathered at each crack in the wall.

We had improved upon our mode of transportation. Instead of the pail, which had a tendency to drag us toward the precipice, we now had haversacks that, strapped to our backs, allowed freedom for our hands. I also found that the small, pointed garden hoe could serve as an ice axe; it had a pointed side, and, when this was well planted in the frozen snow, it helped pull us up.

One afternoon, the snow had ceased falling and the wind had died down slightly. Upon leaving the house, we were all very surprised to see the diffused light of a reddish sun and to notice, on either side, two other suns, not quite so bright. What wasn't so bright was that the thermometer was frozen at forty-seven below zero. You can imagine how we sought the shelter of the creek from the wind! During those two weeks, we lived in a sort of stupor. It must have been the storm's perpetual howling that left us rather dazed. We had become robots, closed in day and night, physically and morally, in this whirlwind of powdered snow.

When, after superhuman efforts each day, we reached the mine, we were surrounded by a great calm. The enormous cliff that formed a sort of protecting wall was our best refuge against the howling wind. Henri and I looked at each other smiling, and Henri said one day:

"We are like troglodytes, cave-dwellers, who, in their day, must have experienced cyclones, hurricanes, and cataclysms of all sorts."

When the time had come to return to work, we both feared the moment when we would leave the shelter of the snowbank on the edge of the ravine more than the climb up the wall. We also had avalanches, but, fortunately, they passed in front or behind us.

Each morning, the thermometer read minus forty-five degrees or close to it. At noon, it might show minus forty. But, everything must end. One day in January, the sun reappeared in the calm of a sky, which now appeared to be of a deeper blue. At two o'clock, the windows began to thaw, and, all at once, it seemed, we noticed that it was daylight until four o'clock in the afternoon, our time. We had planted a long stake on the side of the house at high noon one day and kept checking the length of the shadow.

In early February, we began to wonder about our neighbours. What had become of Seymour and Freer? Had they been able to hold out in their shack? We made a good provision of coal, and, the following day, Henri and I started for their ranch.

We were not too surprised, as we reached the creek and crossed it in a large diagonal, to notice the modifications brought about to the topography by the snowfall and the strong winds of the last two weeks. There were now artificial hills in the most unexpected places, and, in other spots, where the wind had had no hold, we provoked miniature avalanches as we went by. It took us close to two hours for what normally would have been a half-hour walk. We hoped that there might be mail.

Upon arriving at the ranch, Freer, on top of his rack on a hillside facing south, was throwing hay to shaggy-looking cattle with rounded backs. He told us that Seymour had gone to Harringtons' place to get the mail. Henri, who I had introduced, asked about the cattle, which appeared to have suffered. Freer answered that they had lost fifteen head, principally cows that had been too thin, and half the year's crop of calves, that is, about twenty.

"What did you do with them?" I innocently asked.

"The coyotes ate them before they were cold," he answered.

"You have no shelter?" asked Henri.

"How can you build a shelter for wild cattle that can't be tied and that would demolish everything? And, moreover, if we had a barn, how could you possibly get rid of the manure from three hundred head of cattle? It would require five or six men, and that would eat up the profits; the price of one cow is about the salary of a man for one month!"

"I don't see your horses. Did they perish also?"

"They surely didn't. In fact, they've never been so fat! And, how is the old gentleman?"

"Oh, he's quite well," replied Henri, "but I think he would feel a whole lot better were he to receive news from the old country."

"Well, why don't you go in, make yourselves some tea, warm yourselves up a bit. I'll be there shortly."

We added wood to the fire and put the kettle on. When our host returned, his beard loaded with icicles, he had to lean over the stove to thaw it out and detach it from the collar of his sheepskin jacket, to which it was frozen. Then, he seized an enormous piece of beef from a cupboard, cut three huge slices, the size of my two fists, which he fried in the big frying pan, and added the contents of a can of tomatoes, which in the end he covered with liquid pimento-mustard. He covered the whole thing up. I had the feeling that we were really going to be warmed up!

There was no bread. Apparently, the dough had completely refused to rise, so we made dough biscuits using baking powder. This didn't bother us much since it was our habitual menu. While we were eating, and after, as he smoked numerous pipes, Freer told us that, having twice attempted to enter the Royal Cadet Navy School and having twice failed, he had come to Canada. As to his pal, we were discreetly told that he had come to this country to forget an ill-fated love affair.

When Seymour returned, his horse was all covered with snow and its rump was steaming. The horseman was frozen, and he had a hard time talking because his cheeks were white with cold. He threw us the bag holding the mail. What a joy to see, on the envelopes, mother's handwriting, and Jean's. There was a letter from Belgium for Henri, and another from his friend Domenech in St. Boniface.

We couldn't stay much longer, as nightfall was fast approaching. While we were walking, Henri had opened his letter and was reading for me. A terrible winter in Belgium: nineteen below at Soignies! Bah! thought I, that's good weather! Everyone was in good health, including Bonnevie, who had met my mother and Jean twice in Brussels. (My God! How far away this all seemed to me.) In St. Boniface, the college had opened up again, but not completely. Later that night, when Father had read the letters, he said:

"It's a good thing that they don't suspect what went on here. We'll tell them about it later, little by little; but they, too, are courageous and that is comforting for us. . . . Yes, my children, your mother is an admirable woman, and, when Jean gets here, I am sure he won't be the last to pitch in. In six or seven weeks, they should be approaching this continent."

The days were getting longer now. One morning, through the window, we could see small fluffy clouds coming toward us from the west. Outside, we could feel a rather warm breeze coming up from the valley.

"That's the Chinook!" said Henri. "It's a sign that spring isn't very far off!"

That night, the Chinook left us and a new wave of cold struck again. It seemed as if some evil genius, a Master of the icy North surprised by the Chinook, had suddenly become furious! Another blizzard grudgingly began to persecute us. As a consolation, we said to one another:

"That's probably the last storm!"

How little did we know. . . .

Around 20 March, Master Chinook, having no doubt secured reinforcements, led an all out attack against General Winter. This time, his strategy was successful. For three days, the wind blew from the west south-west, and, one morning, the soil reappeared. For five months, it had been shrouded. . . . We still had our doubts, but, this time, it was true. The sun became much warmer, and the snow disappeared completely after two weeks.

One day, during the thaw, Joseph de Bailleux arrived.

He had gained weight. He always smiled and always dangled a cigarette.

"This time, that's it! It's the spring thaw! You're not sick are you? I've brought the mail; that should cheer you up."

There were four letters from the family. When my father had read the most recent he exclaimed:

"Well, children, they're on their way. Aren't we the twenty-seventh today?"

"No, it's the twenty-fifth," answered Joseph.

"That's possible, . . . but our passengers are supposed to be in Halifax on the thirtieth. They are presently at sea. Two or three days at Musy's, . . . then twice as long to reach Stettler. . . . We might all be reunited around 8 or 10 April! It's time we got the house ready. We shall need a team of horses to haul the materials."

"I've just heard that Foot is selling out. The winter completely discouraged him, and he has decided to go up to Edmonton to work at his trade. Apparently, things are booming there. There are two mares, a young stallion, two sets of harness, a saddle; his other saddle horse, which you know, died last month. There's also a wagon with a box and rack, a sleigh, a mower, and a rake. I've taken upon myself to ask him to wait until I had seen you. The price is good. He agreed to wait."

"Good. Can you pick me up one of these days?"

"Tomorrow, if you wish," said our friend.

What had been said was done, and that night the deal had been swung. As we were returning with the wagon hitched to the two mares and me riding Fred the stallion (a beautiful horse in spite of his furry black mane), guess who caught up with us in the hills between Harringtons' and the big crest? Baptiste himself, who, full of ardour and good will, came to offer his help to build the barn. Upon seeing our equipment he exclaimed:

"Batèche! Father Durieux, you are surely set up now! Three good horses and your two boys there; things are going to roll from now on!" . . .

The peace between us had been signed, and, as a token, father offered Baptiste a cigar and also one to Henri. The next day, work began.

We crossed the creek where there was a good spruce

bluff. I must acknowledge that, when Baptiste really decided to work, he could cut a mean swath. When we had circled the creek by the plateau above and tackled the trees, they did not offer much resistance to the axe of the Métis. We could see that he had a lot of experience at this sort of work.

"All you boys have to do is to cut off the branches and pull out the logs with the horses. I'll take care of supplying you with work!"

At nightfall, twenty-five logs had been dragged up near the sleigh. We loaded eight and drove home.

The next day, we took advantage of the good weather, and, at nightfall, there were fifty more logs. The whole pile was close to where the barn was to be erected, and, with the long lumberman's saw, they were all cut the same length. Baptiste, who only used his axe and a handsaw, carved the ends for mortise and tenon joints.

We then began setting up this sort of big square cage, by laying logs one on top of the other. When our twelve logs were in place, the walls were over two metres high. Then, Baptiste did like Crespel in Hoffman's Tales; he decreed:

"We're going to make the door, right here. We'll put one window there, and another one there!"

We nailed vertical boards on either side where the openings were going to be, and, with the big saw, we cut away at the spruce logs. Henri left for Stettler, from where he returned with windows and lumber for the door and for the roof, whose frame we had already mounted with spruce logs. Thus, our barn was completed, and there was room for three more animals in it, including our horses.

Upon his return, Henri had also brought back a telegram from Montreal, announcing the arrival of the ship in Halifax and mother's stop at Musy's place. The arrival in Stettler was expected eight days after the date on the telegram. . . . Foot came to help us build the stairs that were to become our pathway to go to bed, and a wall was built on the main floor to partition off our parents' bedroom. Finally, when all this was done, we started on our way, stopping by at Noullet's for the night. Henri and my father were in the sleigh, and I was riding Fred, who became restless each time he saw horses in the neighbourhood.

In Stettler, we found Frenchmen who had travelled on

the same boat as mother and Jean. They had not stopped in Montreal and were able to give us news of our travellers. These people came from Roubaix and had taken the boat at Antwerp with Jean, mother, and Bonnevie. Their name was Laisnez; the group consisted of two couples without children and a third brother who was completely different from the other two, who were weavers by trade. The weavers spoke the Roubaix patois with a very strong Flemish accent, whereas the other brother expressed himself in very correct language. Henri, who boasts of being perspicacious and a bit of a philosopher, admitted that he was faced with an enigma. Try as he might to find out by questions or even setting traps for the fellow to fall into, the Laisnez brother would smile and shrewdly avoid answers. He didn't give himself away! They had bought two horses and a wagon and had decided to accompany us toward the Red Deer in order to find three quarter sections of land.

The long-awaited day finally arrived! What an unforgettable moment was the one when we fell into each other's arms! Jean and mother were surprised at how much I had grown and how strong and bronzed I was. We spoke about friend Musy, who had never answered my father's letters but who had been very kind to my mother without mentioning what had taken place in July. She was rather tired from the long trip. This I could see in her eyes, but a kind of exaltation prompted her to hurry our departure. We tried to tell her that there still was a lot of snow, even though we weren't sorry, since we had been able to use the sleigh. The Laisnezs, too, wanted to be on their way. It took Rossé's reasonable arguments to convince them to be patient. Bonnevie was still too groggy from his trip. Big papa Stettler was extremely gentlemanly. Boulot, who had returned from Red Deer, had been put in charge by my father and took on a busy air. The natural grace of my mother and her tactfulness had literally revolutionized all of Stettler, and the toughest Yankee became extremely polite in the hotel lobby when the French lady went by. In the meantime, Jean had gone with Henri to the Red Deer land office and had filed a homestead claim by signing Marcel Durieux. . . . Finally, one night, Joseph de Bailleux arrived with his two best horses hitched on to a brand new buggy, announcing that the road was passable. We could leave the next morning, but he wanted the honour of driving Mrs. Durieux. This was agreed to, and the procession, or, rather, the caravan, was organized. In my quality as a nine-month-old westerner, I took the lead on Fred who, from time to time, whinnied as a sort of triumphal trumpet! Then followed the buggy with Joseph and my mother, then the sleigh, with father, Henri, Jean, the baggage, and the provisions . . . and, finally, the Laisnez wagon, the women having stayed in Stettler. We had warned the Laisnezs not to follow the sleigh tracks because wagons and sleighs don't follow the same contours. At first, they followed our instructions very well; but, as we arrived in the hills, they lost track of us from time to time. I had to go back and set up our red lanterns for them to see. Jules Laisnez swore not to let go of our tracks in the snow for fear of becoming lost. When the tracks were on the slope of a hill, the sleigh got by easily, but the wagons slid until a large stone would suddenly stop them, . . . risking shattering the wheels or tipping the wagon. Father advised Henri to go and take over. It was a welcome solution, and we were able to advance normally. As far as Joseph was concerned, he had gone on ahead in order not to prolong mother's trip.

At night, we were at the Noullets'. The Laisnezs set up their tent with our help, and Henri and Jean went to sleep at another Frenchman's home at the Lourdels, five kilometres away, toward Lowden Lake. I shared the tent with the people from Roubaix and noticed that, for three-quarters of an hour, the bachelor Laisnez was absent before returning to bed down by himself in a corner.

The next day, around ten o'clock, it was Hubert de Bailleux who returned with his dashing team to drive mother. They took such a lead that, when we finally arrived home, Hubert and mother had almost finished preparing our supper. This was really the true housewarming! Boulot had also arrived so that there were ten of us around the table . . . nine men, and one precious lady. Eight of us were from the north of France, one from Béarne, and one from Burgundy, which in itself represented quite a French triangle. Mother found everything superb and marvellous and even more beautiful than the sketch I had sent her. The bachelor Laisnez joined the party and surprised us with his pertinent considerations and profound observations. After the supper, Boulot returned home, Hubert came to sleep with us in the loft of the house, and the Laisnezs went back to their tent.

The following Sunday, it was Mr. Lourdel from Lowden Lake who came to visit. He rode a small Arab horse. Here, once more, we were able to admire a beautiful horseman. In spite of his fifty-four years, he had a great deal of control and ability. He had fought in the Kabylie area of Africa in 1873 and knew what it was to go up mountains without ever having to walk. On the other hand, if he was a good horseman, he wasn't much of an orator, although he did try. He always mixed Arab words with his speech, especially when he spoke English. The kind man was also like our friend Musy: he had his own definite ideas, and he was always at odds with one or two people in his large family (he had a daughter married to a Mr. Harlet, two sons, and two other daughters) or else he became embroiled with a neighbour. For the moment, it was with Mr. Noullet. As father inquired about raising horses in central Alberta, this is the type of answer he got:

"As for raising horses, Mr. Durieux, I have to tell you that it is a task that is not given to each one to understand. For example, in this country here, near the Red Deer, you can't expect to proceed like in France at Dury in the Pas-de-Calais, ... where, for a while, I raised Anglo-Arabs for light cavalry, because, in the end, what they were looking for, as for example, when I was in Kabylie at Haras de Blidah where there were Spahis, if you breed horses that are too heavy well, then, they have breathing problems. ... All this is to say, Mr. Durieux, that saddle horses and draught horses are very different. You will tell me that, in the Prairies here, the Indian ponies can do both jobs; ... it's like Percherons; ... they are as good at field work as at pulling wagons. ... If you were to cross them with the local ponies, they would breed good saddle horses. Yet, you have the Americans who think they are so smart, well they haven't succeeded" ... etc., etc., ... and this continued for hours!

He was a fine old man but a little tiring in the end. Henri had switched the conversation to politics, but even so our good papa Lourdel attacked everyone: the Free-Masons, the Jews, the Dreyfusards, the Panamists, and the anti-militarists, of which he made an unbelievable salad!

However, we had to consider practical things. Now that our buildings were up, we had to think of opening land for our first crop. In Canada, people refer to this as "breaking" land. Three horses were hitched on the plow that we had bought in

Stettler, and we began to turn the sod and, here and there, a few roots of willow or wild roses. We had obtained seed potatoes, and, when we had gone over the breaking with the disk and harrow, we sowed the potatoes and a bit of barley . . . total, about one and a half hectars (close to four acres). Then, I was off to Boulot's to give him a hand. It was quite different from our land. His was forested, and only one-quarter of his land was prairie. There were two large sloughs. I had taken along Bonnevie's gun and was able to shoot a few ducks. I helped clear some land, put up fences, and fix up the house. When I later returned home, father mobilized me for the garden, where we planted all sorts of vegetables. Mother had now fully recovered from her trip and had taken on the task of sewing and mending. Jean, who had purchased a beautiful double-barrelled shot-gun, succeeded in bringing home quite a few prairie chickens. This was good, because we had no more frozen meat and we couldn't get any at this time. We had bought laying hens, and omelettes and bacon and eggs were often on the menu. The moment arrived when we tasted our own radishes, lettuce, peas, beets; . . . you can well imagine how proud we were. We even thought the vegetables had a very special taste of their own, especially those of us who had wintered on dry beans and rice! In the field, the potatoes and barley were growing fast; it seemed as if nature, which had been compressed during five months, wanted to make up for lost time. In the same manner, hundreds of birds had come up from the south; robins and orioles whose whistling was completely different from that of their European cousins. On the open prairie, flowers of all sorts, with soft or bright colors, grew everywhere, especially tiger lilies and little blue-bells.

In June, we bought twelve cows, four of which had calves. We put them down by the creek and cut off the ravines with short fences. There were five more cows who were ready to calve and one, not too wild, that we could milk. We bought a piglet who became so tame that he followed my father everywhere in company with the dog and cat. In July, the dairy cow gave birth to a calf, and we had all the milk we needed. My father succeeded in making his first butter, and we had cottage cheese as well. In mid-July, we ate our first new potatoes. With this good weather, mother succeeded in making very tasty bread and all sorts of pastry. In the meantime, Henri had gone to get two more loads of lumber, in order to enlarge the house. As Foot was in Edmonton, we hired a Stettler carpenter who, in three days, with our help, put up a new room in front of the older building, which became our kitchen, the old kitchen now becoming the parlour. We bought a small coal stove to heat up the rooms. Everything seemed to be going very well. Mother, however, seemed to tire easily.

One day, we saw a new type of locomotion. It consisted of a one-horse buggy, as seen in cities. Usually on the open prairie, the heavy wagons are hitched to two horses, and, because of this, roads are made in two parallel tracks. These tracks wind along, avoiding stones, stumps, and holes. You can see that a country horse used to these trails, when hitched by himself, will naturally follow the track and that the buggy will automatically ride on the sides! So much so that the two passengers who were approaching were feeling the bumps, to which they seemed to have adapted. When they got closer, we recognized one of the passengers. It was Father Renut, from Trochu, but the other bearded gentleman was completely unknown to us; . . . he was almost as strange as the buggy. Father Renut, a brave and saintly man, was known for his good humour and his kindliness. When he used to visit us, always on horseback, with his small suitcase in the back of his saddle, we were doubly happy to receive our pastor and our friend. With a big, broad, triumphant smile, he now jumped out of the rig, in spite of his forty-five years, and proclaimed in a solemn tone:

"My friends, I am greatly honoured to be able to introduce my new means of transportation; . . . my dignified posterior not being able to put up with a Mexican saddle anymore, I now require a carriage! This carriage, I must say, is not mine. It belongs to 'Monsieur the Count of Bouville'."

Upon these words, the gentleman in question got up as if pushed by a spring, and, at the same time, as he was preparing to bow solemnly, his horse, tempted by a tuft of green grass, brusquely pulled ahead so much so that the posterior of the driver Count joined the spot it had just left. Father Renut raised the horse's head and said to it:

"You see where your gluttony has led you!"

"Yes Dan," said M. de Bouville, "you make me sit down before a lady who is standing, which is extremely ill-mannered, you know. Please accept my apologies Madam."

My mother then went forward in her simple, gracious way and extended her hand to the seated Count.

"Allow me to come down, Madam."

Then, having set foot on the ground, he bowed very low over the grass, and, rising with majesty, he touched mother's hand with his bearded lips.

Father Renut declared that M. the Count of Bouville, from the old nobility of the south-west of France, an authentic cadet from Gasconny, and an aging bachelor, had come to seek a fortune and, perhaps, a wife in Canada. (It certainly wasn't the place, because there was one woman for every six men in this part of the country.)

"I had the misfortune," continued the Father, "of seeing my horse wounded at the hoof, but, on the other hand, divine providence made me fall into the buggy of M. de Bouville, who wanted to prospect between Stettler and the river. It was on my way, and the three of us form a model trio . . . the Count, Dan, and myself. We walk, if I may say so, hand in hand. As our load is fairly heavy, in the hills, the bipeds get down and help the quadruped with their voice and gestures. On the sharp slopes, everybody gets down, including Dan, who slides on his rump!"

In spite of his facetious remarks, Father Renut was not exaggerating at all. One day, I travelled with them, and the trip I took was worth it. The Count, for example, upon seeing from far off a big stone well stuck between the two tracks of the road, would start talking to his horse in advance.

"Dan! Dan! My rabbit! You see that big stone, don't you? Please do not run over it. Look, Father, look, he's going to go right over it! Aie! Aie! The bandit! You'll see how I shall feed you! . . . I won't give you anything to eat or to drink!"

You may well conclude that Father Renut had his distractions during his trips around the country.

As our home was now finished, Mother asked Father Renut to bless it. The next morning, mass was celebrated for the first time. This was quite a different environment from the services we had attended in Quebec, in Manitoba, or in Red Deer and Stettler. Within these walls, which had been the witnesses of our terrible and anguishing winter, there was now an assembled family, . . . and the prayers which we said were full of confidence and hope. One year ago, here, there were nothing but coyotes who furtively went by in the night and partridge and prairie chickens who fled like arrows in the sky. Mother, who was a devout Catholic and close to a mystic, declared to us after this mass that she considered it to be the most edifying she had ever attended. As all the Durieuxs had good voices, we sang the Royal Mass. We could see that Father Renut wasn't too used to this type of accompaniment. This might explain why, in the future, Father rearranged his itinerary and made more frequent trips to our home. In the afternoon, our friends Seymour and Freer came over and respectfully greeted Father Renut. They explained that, in the morning, the wind had carried our voices and they had heard a religious hymn . . . so much so that Freer had taken the liberty of bringing his guitar. We were surprised by this gesture toward more friendly relations on the part of our neighbours. Mother could speak English fairly well, and her great understanding of people could only attract the respects of bachelors who were well mannered. Seymour, in spite of his physique, which we could compare to that of Lord Kitchener, was very timid and, at first, could only stutter in answer to the friendly questions my mother asked. Little by little, he opened up, and we noticed that he had a very generous and sensitive nature. Thanks to music, an international language, our social relations improved greatly. We had some printed music and so did Freer. Toward the end of the evening, we already had a fairly good concert going.

Father Renut had also enjoyed his mass, at which we all sang. He decided to stay the next morning rather than leave for Ewing. That greatly pleased mother, who thought that the ceremony was like those celebrated by Christians in the early years of the Church, when they were persecuted and had to hide in far-away places! Mother, as we understood much later, had a great need for spiritual comfort. She must have completely sacrificed her own personal tastes and comforts to adapt to this new form of life, so far removed and completely opposed to her education and her life as a young girl and happy bride. And, here, I saw another proof of the power of the spirit over matter. We never heard one single complaint from her about the conditions of life in Western Canada. We had, later on, more frequent services, and what follows will tell you the reason why.

You remember, perhaps, that I mentioned the Laisnez

family, the "Roubaix people" as we used to call them? We saw them arrive one afternoon, and the eldest, who always spoke solemnly and yet in a funny way because he expressed himself in a jargon that was a mixture of the patois of the Franco-Belgian border, announced that they had decided to file for three homesteads four kilometres to the south-east. They had even started to cut logs in order to build a big house where, at first, they would all live together. When he had finished, the character who had so intrigued us by his enigmatic ways rubbed his hands unctuously and said, smiling maliciously:

"Mrs. Durieux, Sir, my friends, I would be loathe to prolong any further the equivocal situation that I believed I had to adopt at the beginning of our relationship. We arrived here as unknowns and pioneers, and we needed freedom. Now that I am about to become your neighbour, I want to inform you, personally, of my true identity. I am a priest, a college professor, who, for reasons of health and over-exertion, was forced to completely change his manner of living. I hope to build up my physical and moral strength. You have probably noted a difference in the level of education between my brothers and me. It is due to the generosity of a notable of our native parish of Roubaix. This allowed me, after my primary schooling, to enter a college for my secondary training. After graduation, I went to the great seminary at Cambrai to end up, in the first stage, as a professor at the College of Our Lady of Grace, at Roubaix. I finally became Prefect of Studies. After three years of work under this heavy load, I found myself in such a state of depression one day that the faculty advised me to completely abandon all activities and to have a complete change of life for a period of at least two years. At that time, my brothers had almost decided to emigrate, tempted by the advantages offered to them in Canada. I joined them, hoping to regain my strength on this continent. My brothers, in their youth, were farmers, and, thanks to your advice and that of friendly neighbours, we hope to find, . . . for them, a means of living . . . and, for me, health."

I must admit that after this speech we were all a little confused, especially those of us who hadn't been too shy to make nasty remarks about this person! Henri apologized rather nicely. The priest smiled and, to relax us, told a funny story. From that day on, Father Laisnez was able to act openly, and, from then on, we became close friends.

We had also made the acquaintance of the other French families of Lowden Lake and Ewing where we found people from almost every region of France. People from Morvan, Vendée, Lyon, Flanders, and Artois. As a whole, they were more pleasant than those we had met in the parish of Our Lady of Lourdes in Manitoba. The proverb, birds of a feather flock together, must be true.

VII

Prairie fires and the first death

    At home, our primitive pasture soon proved too small to feed eleven cows and eight calves, not counting the horses. We now had five. We had to think about letting them graze on the open range. Therefore, we applied for a brand at the provincial office in Calgary, for the UT/SL to apply on the right hind leg of our cattle. As far as our horses were concerned, we inherited the Seymour brand, which was an SL mark on the left front shoulder. When we had secured the branding irons, forged by the blacksmith in Stettler, we had to prepare for our first "branding." The two de Bailleux brothers came over to initiate us to this operation, which is indispensable in this country, where cattle roam in freedom on vacant lands during eight months of the year. We built a strong corral of poles, modelled on Seymour's but smaller. At an angle to this corral, we had a smaller, round one, about ten metres across, with a huge, five-foot-high post in the centre. The animal is first isolated, so that two of them are not lassoed at the same time, and, when the slip-knot is around the animal's neck, the other end of the rope is twined around the post. The cow, calf, or bull, half out of breath, opposes with less and less resistance, and soon, little by little, it is drawn up to the post, . . . or almost, on its knees. At the same moment, two strong men roll it on its side while its two hind legs are tied in the loop of a lasso prepared beforehand. Then, the second lasso is suddenly pulled, and the animal is stretched out, tied by the neck and the hind legs. Care must be taken so that the animal falls on the opposite side to the one that has to be marked.

During this operation, the irons are heated, a helper passes them through the fence openings, another fellow holds on to the neck and the horns, one holds the animal by sitting on its belly, and a third one on the hind legs, . . . and, the first time, we close our eyes because applying a red-hot iron on the skin of a living animal is cruel; but, necessity commands. The scar heals quickly without complications, so much so that we become accustomed to this operation, which at first seems so barbaric.

Branding also has a sporty side. As in bullfights, the savage beast and man find themselves face to face, and it is clear that these manoeuvres, which appear so simple on paper, never really take place without someone receiving some kind of a blow or scratch or kick. The experienced cowboys, which we were not at the time, work exclusively on horseback to roll the animals over. Years later, another system, that of chutes, was invented, with one fixed wall and one moveable, which allowed many operations, such as branding and vaccinating, at the same time.

After the branding was over, we had to take care of haying. This was done on free land. One section on two was reserve land belonging to the CPR, the Hudson's Bay, or the schools. As a rule, these lands remained free for five or six years after the last homestead had been taken in the region. This time lapse was usually sufficient to allow the settler to increase his holdings. In these open spaces, the hay belonged to the first come. The first occupant, in this case, was the one who made a first cut with his mower around the field, but, because of abuse, it had been decided that the first cut by the mower could not exceed in surface area more than two mowers could mow in one day. Credit must be given to the ranchers of our district, because this custom was never broken. On our part, in order to keep up with the tradition of Seymour and Freer, we went to ask them which areas they wanted to keep for their own use. Before beginning our work, we had built a slider that, with the help of horses, would allow us to put up twenty tons of hay per day.

The Laisnezs had bought a mower, but, as they owned neither rake nor slider, we co-operated during the haying season. In order to cut this fine hay, we had to wait until the dew was completely gone. Our blades had to be as sharp as razors, and, because we operated in virgin territory, there were constant obstacles—stones, stumps, gopher holes, bones—so many that we couldn't work for more than two hours. With two mowers, that made eight blades to sharpen each day. The rate of work in the West is almost infernal! That's a necessity, because the season lasts only from 15 April until 15 October, and the frost-free mornings last from 15 May to 15 September. Between sowing, which must be done before June, summer fallow, which has to be harrowed later, haying in mid-July, cutting wheat, stooking, threshing, and, in between, building barbed wire fences, for which we had to cut, sharpen, and plant fence posts (not always easy to find), there was no time to waste. When I think that we had to put up forty-five kilometres of fences with three wire strands, . . . and that does not include the land Jean bought later, . . . the numerous rolls of barbed wire we had to unroll, . . . the clamps which had to be nailed in, . . . and that, in spite of that, we had to spend one fifth of our time watching and repairing all this; . . . indeed, there was no time for loafing!

When the haystacks and stacks of green feed were finished, they still had to be surrounded, at a distance, by ten or twelve furrows made by a plow, in order to protect them against possible prairie fires, which are the plague of autumn and early spring. I saw one of those on a Sunday afternoon as Freer and Seymour were having tea with us.

In the north-east, we noticed a high, mushroom-like, rusty cloud, unnatural in a cloudless sky. Seymour took on a worried look and murmured a little louder than usual.

"Hm! Hm! Looks like a prairie fire to me. We'd better go and take a look."

We saddled the horses and picked up old gunny sacks fixed to big cudgels, which, by the way, were ready and kept for that purpose, and we galloped toward the high hills that shut off our horizon, six kilometres away.

When we reached the high point dividing the two slopes and the whole bend in the Big Valley appeared before us, the rusty cloud was twice as high and four times as wide.

"There's no immediate danger for us," said Freer, "the valley creek with its long green grass will cut the fire ahead; but, should the wind increase, new points can form and follow the flat where the grass is dry and hasn't been cut."

From all directions, groups of riders now appeared. A compact group of about fifteen men, led by the Ewing Postmaster, arrived at full gallop. He organized the men on the spot. On a three-kilometre front, six riders went up and down the creek to prevent any surprises, whereas all the other volunteers forded the creek to fight the fire in a more dangerous area. The damned wind was blowing stronger.... Toward the north-east, we had seen a long chain of men busy trying to turn the fire toward a body of water connected to Lowden Lake. We had no worries from that side.

Three points had formed where we were fighting. One of them climbed the first hill on the other side of the valley and seemed to advance at the speed of a trotting horse. It was no use getting any closer. A group of hardy and vigorous young men kept the edges of the fire in check to prevent it from spreading. The second point, advancing in a depression where the wind had little effect, was promptly put out, but the third one gave us a great deal of trouble due to burning dried willow stumps that gave up an unbearable amount of heat. Sudden squalls carried burning coals as far as fifty metres. A tough fight ensued, and, in the choking smoke, each one was on his own as the fire rekindled itself everywhere around us. Fortunately, the riders from the south, who by then had checked the fire from their side, arrived in time to help us, proving once again the close solidarity that existed among all the settlers.

We were all exhausted. Our eyes were burning, our throats parched, and our pant legs nothing but ashes. Other farmers from north of Lowden Lake had started a counter-fire along the trail leading to the Hand Hills. By sunset, the fire out there was checked, and, by nightfall, only the stumps of bushes glowed intermittently in the night breeze. Our horses raised clouds of ashes as we returned home dead-tired and looking like chimney sweeps. Jean and I went out again in the middle of the night to check. We could smell the burnt grass everywhere and see hundreds of glowing specks in the night. This, we found out, was dried cow manure, which burnt until late the next day.

The following autumn, we were to have another bout with fire. We had almost started one and only our quick reactions prevented a catastrophe.

One afternoon, during a strong wind, we were busy loading a wagon with willow fence poles, when Henri, bending to pick up an armful, dropped burning tobacco from his pipe. Instantaneously, the grass caught fire! In seconds, the flames bounced steps ahead and spread out. Close by were tree branches with leaves still on them. With these, the three of us began to pursue the fire. Eyebrows and eyelashes burning, we succeeded in creating a deviation toward a depression between two bushes protected from the wind. We finally put out the last flame around a huge badger hole. There were haystacks all around, and we shuddered at the thought of what might have been.

In the heart of the winter of 1909-10, a huge fire destroyed part of the town of Stettler. On a windy night, an over-heated stove set fire to an unprotected ceiling. It was around half-past ten. At one o'clock in the morning, three-quarters of the town was up in flames, the sparks having crossed a sixty-foot street. The only area spared was the block on which stood papa Stettler's hotel. People had to be billetted in farm homes ten miles around the town.

Toward the end of autumn, a welcomed inheritance allowed us to purchase ten year-and-a-half-old calves. The large quantity of hay we had put up helped us to feed them through the winter months and prepare them for market the following year. The Laisnezs, who also had plenty of hay, had bought a great many dairy cows, built a log barn, and decided to produce milk and butter all winter. This was not normal practise in an area where ranchers bought condensed milk in cans from November to April. Only around cities had dairies been established, where the buildings were heated. The milk had to be shipped in a thermos-type container.

The Reverend Laisnez had also taken a homestead. He appeared to have decided to remain in the country for a few years. Early that winter, we noticed that the good priest was very sensitive to the cold, and he had the colour of tuberculosis patients. As his condition worsened, he became very detached from all ideas of comfort, personal satisfaction, and well-being. My mother also suffered and, in spite of her courage, considered herself an apprentice compared to this master of stoicism. The priest had first attempted to live by himself in a small house on his quarter, but, at the end of February, he had to admit that he could no longer live alone. His brothers prepared a small room in their home for him. Dr. Authenec, who, between crises of his own, had examined the priest, confided to my parents that, humanly speaking, there was nothing more his medicine could do. He lasted through the winter, and even the miracle of the Canadian spring did little, although he did seem to improve slightly. A book on the Kneip method of treatment had fallen into the hands of Emile Laisnez (Senior), who decided, in desperation, to try it on their poor patient, who accepted with docility the rude trials of this method as developed by the Bavarian priest. My parents, who one day had attended one of those cruel sessions, had tried to put a stop to it, but the priest, totally resigned, stated that he wanted to try the full treatment. My brother Henri was so exasperated that, without asking anyone's permission, he brought Dr. Donovan from Stettler, who categorically forbade the treatment, which was barbaric and useless.

Toward the end of September, the very thin priest, who had lost all his strength and had reached the limit of his endurance, passed away, attended by Father Renut. The family was completely bereaved and had a difficult time getting over this loss.

In the small log room, on a fragile camp-bed covered with a rough brown blanket, I imagined a martyr brought back from the catacombs after torture. I saw in mother's eyes that she was thinking the same thing, . . . and, as we came out of the room, she said, her eyes glowing with a mystic look:

"Did you see how calm he was and that triumphant look? . . . I feel that he has already received his reward; . . . now he sees . . . now he knows!"

The grave was dug on Jules Laisnez's homestead. It was placed between two small hills, against a willow bush whose leaves were almost blue. After the funeral mass, by Father Bazin of Trochu, the rough pine coffin was lowered and Father Renut said the last prayers. Around the open grave, there were neighbours and at least one representative from each French family for thirty kilometres around. Among them was a good Norwegian who could not hide his grief and cried openly. The small children were wide-eyed before this unaccustomed spectacle, especially when the grave was filled.

As I left the house where he had died, I instinctively turned toward this corner of land where the first burial of all this region had been held, and I felt a tightening in my chest because I had painfully surprised a look in my mother's eyes, something like envy, as she glanced upon the last resting place of her model of courage and resignation. . . .

VIII

The parents pass on

Let us turn back the calendar slightly to the Christmas of the preceding year and the memorable night during which many of us almost froze to death on the hills west of Lowden Lake.

We had attended midnight mass at Mr. Lourdel's home. After the ceremony, he had treated us to a magnificent "réveillon," which lasted until two o'clock in the morning. We then prepared to leave. Upon reaching the stable, we noticed that a blizzard was already in full force. Snow bit the lanterns like luminous sand. Brice Boulot, who that winter was staying at the Randons', muttered as he bent his high frame to tie the traces to the whipple tree of the sleigh.

"What an excuse for weather! It won't be easy to approach the Noullets' with the storm blowing in our faces."

The two de Bailleuxs and Fournier, well seated in their cutter and wrapped in all sorts of blankets and furs and having taken a few shots of whisky, acted sure of themselves. Mr. Noullet climbed up on the lead sleigh with Boulot, the Randons, and Father Renut, who hadn't eaten because he had to say mass at Noullets' that morning. Harlet, Lourdel's son-in-law, rode another sleigh with his wife, Simeon, and Martha (his brother-in-law and his sister). Jean, my brother, was riding Buck, our new saddle horse, and I was riding Fred, who was completely subdued by the wind and storm.

After we had abandoned the precarious tracks leading to a haystack and had passed the last of Lourdel's gates, partly hidden in a snowbank, we drove in a sort of snowy corridor between two phantom hills, whose crests smoked like volcanoes. All the teams, whipped by a front wind, constantly tried to turn around and go home. That was our loss. We had no horses belonging to Fournier or Noullet, who could have found their way back to their own stables.

Fred was following the track painfully opened by the team ahead. Mr. Noullet, turning toward me, shouted above the wind:

"I'm afraid this won't work! . . . The hills are all the same; . . . we'll have to keep heading into the wind."

Usually the wind blew from the north-west, but the damned blizzard had decided to lose us and constantly seemed to turn. Our tactics failed, and, after half an hour of painful progress, which we believed to be in a straight line, we crossed our own previous trail at right angles. We were in the shelter of two hills and we stopped. I felt some kind of disarray within the group. Naturally, among Frenchmen, we began arguing! Father Renut, sensing the futility of our behaviour, put a stop to it by imposing silence, . . . and Jean, always ready to volunteer, proposed the following:

"You say, Mr. Noullet, that we are about three kilometres from your place; . . . you are sheltered here; . . . why don't you stay here while I go ahead with my horse. It's young and fast. I'll find the trail, and, with a little luck, I should be back in a short while. Don't move away from here so that I can find you."

"O.K.," said Mr. Noullet. "If you can find the southeast point of the large slough on my homestead, cross it. There's a fence on the other side. You can follow it up to the gate on the road to Stettler."

Jean knew the area. He left but didn't return that night; however, he didn't die. (His destiny called him to a more glorious end . . . on the slopes of Mort-Homme at Verdun during the night of 30 April 1916). After two hours of searching, Jean had attained his objective, but both he and the horse were exhausted. After a short rest, he asked that Noullet's horse be saddled, but the racer, rather a frisky beast, absolutely refused to move.

By this time, we knew that something was amiss, and we couldn't stay put anymore. The blood was freezing in our veins. The de Bailleuxs decided to take the lead and headed in approximately a north-westerly direction. The blizzard was still more hostile (if that is possible). Each time we reached the crest of a hill, we were forced to turn our back to the wind, and the horses, taking advantage, would try to head in another direction in order to find shelter. Around four-thirty in the morning, we had to admit that it was useless to continue. The Randon, de Bailleux, and Harlet horses thought only of piling together in order to keep warm. Icicles thirty centimetres long were hanging from their nostrils. Fred, on the other hand, the moment I let go of his reins, would immediately adopt a fixed direction, which, had we followed it, would have at least brought us back to the stable and his mares.

Father Renut's strength was failing; ... we hadn't even a candy to give him and not a drop of whisky. How stupid of us to have forgotten! However, the smokers in the group had matches. While we were massaging the priest's legs to activate his circulation, the other members of the group found an old dead tree protruding from the snow. There was hay and straw in the sleighs and even an old pan used to feed oats to the horses. After repeated attempts, using tiny branches of the dead wood, we finally got a fire going, upon which we gradually piled larger and larger branches and, finally, the larger birch log that, in the end, gave us flames three feet high. When the snow in the pan had melted, we had water, into which we threw small dry leaves found in the hay. Marthe Lourdel gave some of the brew to Father Renut, and we knew he had recovered when he made an awful face and said painfully:

"What an awful taste! That's not good!"

We couldn't help laughing. We asked him if he felt better, and the priest replied that he had not felt anything; ... he remembered nothing!

Around seven in the morning, the storm slackened. Snow had ceased falling and some stars appeared. Finally, the Little Dipper and then the Big Dipper appeared; ... we now had a way of determining our direction, and we continued on our way with new hope. The horses had had a rest and obeyed more readily. I was worried about Jean and prayed and hoped that he had found shelter somewhere.

At the first crack of dawn, we dared look at one another. What a collection of haggard-looking characters we made!

As we came to the top of another hill, Mr. Noullet vaguely recognized the countryside. We had, apparently, drifted three miles in the direction of Big Valley. When dawn finally gave way to full daylight, we were in sight of the Noullet farm.

For Christmas, Alfred Musy, from Montreal, had written to my father.... He seemed to have abandoned all prejudice about Alberta, and his ever-curious temperament prompted him to decide that his next visit would be to the Far West. Unfortunately, his wife passed away prematurely, leaving young children, and we never did see him again. I also had received a letter from Arthur, his eldest son, who intended to visit us, but his father had refused him permission to do so. Toward the middle of February, the second son of Mr. Lourdel, who had once again quarrelled with his father and who had gotten a job driving a team of horses and delivering lumber along the frozen Red Deer River, was the victim of an accident. He was very fortunate not to lose his life.

One evening, while on one of his delivery runs, he felt cold up there on his load and did what every good Canadian driver does in winter . . . he got off and walked alongside the sleigh. He did not notice that water under the snow had seeped up from the river and that his shoes, which were worn, were gradually filling with water. When he became tired of walking, he climbed up again. He couldn't feel his feet anymore, and, a horse having slipped and a rein having come undone, Jean jumped down but fell on his knees, his legs refusing to carry him. He quickly realized that, if he followed the river, he would have to travel for another hour before finding help. He decided to leave his team to try to find help. On his hands and knees, he dragged himself up the high bank to the plateau above, where the chances of finding help were extremely slim. When his eyes reached the level of the plain, he saw a light! A house was there, fifty metres away, and, by a strange coincidence, it belonged to a Swede who knew something about frozen limbs. For one and a half hours, the Swede kept Jean's feet in water mixed with snow and followed this treatment by one hour in cold water and, finally, in lukewarm water. During this time, the Swede's son had gone down the river to find the horses. He was lucky and, in no time, had delivered the load. Four days later, Jean Lourdel arrived at our home, driven by a neighbour of the Swede who had business in Ewing. He was able to walk with the help of two sticks, . . . there were no crutches, and his grey-blue eyes were smiling. As we were all too surprised to speak with this apparition he decided to ask:

"I sure look silly, don't I? You should see my feet!"

While we sat him on the sofa and undid the wrappings around his legs and feet, which were tied with binder twine, he told us his story. His feet were horrible to look at. Yet, surprisingly, in practically no time he was cured and had only a few scars to show for this adventure.

This incident was, for us, another example of the close co-operation that existed among all the settlers at that time. The Swede absolutely refused any remuneration, and, yet, he was destitute.

In the spring, Seymour and Freer left their shack, which bordered on our property, to finish their home on Freer's land in the shelter of a ravine that led to McKenzie Crossing. The access wasn't easy, through coulees and clay hills, . . . but it was nothing compared to the other side of the valley where, to get a load up the hill, eight horses had to be hitched to a wagon.

One day, as I was on my way to see how the two bachelors were progressing, a Chinook was blowing strong. As I reached the crest of the two hills that separated us, I saw, on the snowy surface of the river, wide ribbons of water that made a sort of arabesque design. Two mornings later, we were awakened by prolonged and muffled detonations that came from the bottom of the valley. It was the ice breaking up on the river. The previous spring, we had missed this spectacle. This time, we dressed and hurried down.

In an awful chaos of snow, ice, water, stones, mud, and dead trees, blocks of greenish ice floated about like antediluvian monsters, . . . and, without apparent reason, an unknown force made them crash into each other and sometimes climb over one another to end up in piles and jams so solid that they appeared immovable. But no! Other blocks floated down, slammed into the pile ahead, and, with ferocious obstinacy, succeeded in dislodging the whole thing. Sometimes, in a bend of the river, a dam gradually formed, which plunged into the current in a slow pivoting motion. Sometimes, these jams would hold, and blocks would climb the banks of the river in their blind fury, their sharp edges ripping into huge poplars.

Above the McKenzie ford, one of these haphazard

dams had built up slowly with stumps, branches, roots, and mud. Unfortunately, from the ford itself, nobody had seen this permanent mass that had dammed the creek. The ford was easy to cross. An American named Fletcher, who owned a farm between Boulot's and Michaud's, had seized the occasion of the low creek to move coal from one side of the river to the other. He had already hauled two loads and was proceeding with the third when Mackenzie yelled at him to be careful. Fletcher did not listen or could not hear; . . . the sound of rumbling water suddenly released and roaring down was carried by the walls of the valley. Under the propulsion of new blocks of ice, the dam had let go!

The unfortunate Fletcher saw the liquid mountain, piled high with debris of all sorts and ice flows, appear one hundred steps away from him. Instead of letting go of his team, he tried to save everything, but the river's furore caught up with him before he reached shore. We were all frozen with horror and powerless to help him! Mackenzie, twenty feet away, was trampling his hat with rage. . . . For a second, we saw a wagon wheel and the leg of one of the horses, and that was all. . . . The river did not let go of its prey.

Coal, in appearance so easy to extract, provoked another incident—this one less serious, but, however, it modified the destiny of our friend Seymour.

Some time after the tragedy of McKenzie Crossing, the two Englishmen set out to get a load of coal south of Henri's quarter section, where a vein of excellent quality was now exploited by everyone, without too many precautions being taken for security. As there was a heavy coat of sandstone above the vein, it had gradually become top-heavy, and it was not properly braced. Naturally, it was not those who were responsible for this state of affairs who were its victims. Seymour, having gone in with a shovel to clear the debris, was suddenly caught by the collapse of the ledge above him. The frost must have loosened it. He jumped back but not quite far enough; his left foot was squashed by a block.

When the dust cleared, Freer found his friend kneeling with his head thrown back in pain and almost fainting. With a crowbar, Freer raised the block and pulled Seymour's foot from under. Blood was already flowing freely. Freer made a tourniquet with his handkerchief, tore his shirt, and, with clean moss, made a temporary dressing. The wounded man having come to, Freer loaded him onto the wagon, where, fortunately, there was a pile of hay, and headed for the Harringtons'. He was fairly sure of finding a proper first-aid kit there. In fact a more orthodox dressing was applied, and Seymour was transported to Dr. Donovan's clinic at Stettler in the de Bailleux buggy, which had springs and was much more comfortable than the wagon. The doctor immediately amputated Seymour's big toe and two others as well!

There were no complications. As soon as he could walk with one cane, Seymour left for England where, as if by chance, he found the object of his first love, . . . who had waited for him all this time. They were married, and, the following year, the couple came to Alberta. Seymour became the partner of another Englishman named Powne. For unknown reasons, the partnership dissolved, and the newlyweds returned to England. Freer, who remained by himself on the McKenzie Crossing ranch (which now belongs to Jean Lourdel), often gave us news of the Seymours. The good Englishman, I think, regretted his ranch life. . . .

In the meantime, the small agglomeration around the CPR depot in Stettler was growing. A station had replaced the box car of early days. The town was now taking on airs of a Far-West city (as popularized later by the movies). There were now three parallel streets and four avenues. Another hotel competed with the National, . . . which, however, had the only bar in town. The Trader's Bank had set up offices and amusement halls with billiard tables and bowling alleys and had a numerous clientele. A cinema showed films three days a week, of which a good one-third were of French origin. The comical character of the day was Max Linder. There were three grain elevators and a stock-yard for loading cattle in railroad cars and an enormous drugstore where everything could be found . . . even firearms! People around joked and said:

"If the medicine won't work, you can always use a revolver!"

A town council had been elected and, as its first expense, bought a fire pump. Naturally, a Methodist temple was built, which provoked the building of a Baptist church. This was shared with the Presbyterians. A beautiful school was erected and, finally, a skating rink, which was used all year round for ice-skating in winter and roller-skating in summer. Toward the end of the summer of 1908, work was begun on the Catholic church, and, by Christmas, it was finished.

This church was the occasion of memorable ceremonies for us and of many joyful reunions. The missionaries had mobilized all the talent they could muster in a territory as large as four French departments. The districts of Battle River, Red Deer, Lowden Lake, Big Valley, and Ewing had sent everyone who had some knowledge of music to a first rehearsal. After three days of practise, we had succeeded in setting up, in Stettler, a symphony orchestra, with three violins and one flute, all from Battle River, a clarinet and a cello from Red Deer, two saxophones from Stettler, and my mother played the organ. Jean and I, who could sing a little, took care of the solos. As far as the choir was concerned, it was some sort of melting pot of the Catholic world of central Alberta! By singing in Latin, all of this blended fairly well; in English, it grinded a little, but, for the French hymns, it was unbelievable. What a mixture we were! The main group were French from France, then followed the Belgians and Swiss, and finally the French Canadians and the Métis. There were Irishmen, from Ireland and the United States, and Czechoslovakians, Hungarians, and Poles. When I sang in the choir, upon my right was Swoboda from Pilsen, who worked in the bank, and, on my left, a Métis who was Xavier's nephew from Content. The audience assured us that the ensemble was beautiful! We sang the Mass of the Angels, and I could see people in the congregation singing along with us. When it came time for the French hymn, *Parle, commande et règne!*, I could see Yankee shoes beating time on the floor of the church to this martial tune.

That night, however, the talent was better organized and used. We had given a musical presentation at the Opera House for the new church. Each ethnic group contributed its own folklore instruments: accordions from central Europe, bagpipes, Métis guitars, American banjos, and German harmonicas. The French supplied the symphonic orchestra accompanied by a grand piano. The rhythmic songs of our military marches were greeted by loud whistles that, contrary to the custom in Europe, were a mark of enthusiasm here. The soul behind all this musical organization was the brother of Father Bazin, who had recently arrived from France and had been named parish priest at Stettler. He was a great musician and an excellent tenor. Unfortunately, the parish priest's health failed, and he had to return to France and was replaced in his functions by Father Renut.

The year 1909 was the occasion for a few happy events in the French colony. Marthe Lourdel married one of the Frère brothers, . . . those who had come from France at the same time as us on the *Pomeranian* and who had homesteaded near the Red Deer. The young Miss Frère, who had been so seasick, married a man named Wiart, who was the butcher at Castor, a new station on the CPR extension line, east of Stettler. A young Randon girl married a young man recently arrived from France. There were two births in the Laisnez families. . . .

There was a very cold spell at the beginning of December that year, recalling the year 1906-07 when we arrived. Mother, one day while hanging clothes, lightly froze her thumb. The slight accident unexpectedly became a cause for concern, and the doctor at Stettler was rather surprised upon examining her. The thumb would not heal, and this denoted that mother's health was generally poor. As she had never complained, we had concluded that, with time, it would heal. A few days after Christmas, Father Renut dropped in (much later we supposed that the doctor in Stettler had asked him to), and I shall always remember the look of surprise on his face upon seeing her seemingly well. He became very exuberant and happy, and, on the morning of New Year's Eve, he gleefully announced that he was going to shave off his beard to honour Saint Sylvester!

At first, we thought that this was another one of his jokes, . . . but he was serious. That masculine emblem, it is true, can become extremely uncomfortable in winter when it becomes loaded with icicles. In the summer, it's not much better with the dust and heat; . . . too much time is lost keeping it clean. The good father proceeded to shave it off, and, when he appeared before us, we were aghast. We couldn't recognize him! Playing the game further and changing his voice and posture, it was a truly different man who performed before us. Henri, who was always ready to play tricks on anyone, saw how this could be put to use.

The next day, New-Year's-Day mass was to be at Dr. Authenec's. Henri came out with this bright idea:

"Father, why don't you arrive at the Authenecs' tomorrow, pretending to be someone else, another priest. We could spread the rumour that you were replacing Father Renut in his duties and that he had been called somewhere else. What do you say?"

"Well," thought the priest, "the doctor is very depressed. It might not be a bad thing to make them all laugh a little."

The next day, when we arrived, assuming rather shy attitudes, the young people at the Authenecs' fell right into our trap.

"Where's Father Renut?"

We simply made evasive signs and didn't say too much. In the house, the greetings were short because we had a difficult time controlling ourselves. Mass was said without anyone suspecting anything. It was only later, when we were all eating, that Father Renut stood up and, hiding the lower part of his face with his hand, burst out laughing in his customary way. This created a real "coup de théâtre!" The doctor himself couldn't stop laughing; . . . it was probably his last good laugh because his heart attacks became more frequent during the two months which followed and he passed away in March, a victim of his illness.

The year had begun sorrowfully for our colony. At that time, a series of frightening snowstorms marked winter's last attacks. A neighbour of the Boulets, an elderly German who was on his way to our place to get frozen meat, had trouble with his team along the way. He stopped and found one of the traces had come undone and was dragging in the snow. He removed his mitts and must have kept them off too long, for, when he arrived at our place and shook hands with Henri, my brother knew that his hands were frozen. They were like those of a marble statue. The long treatment, learned from Lourdel's experience, began. As the fingers touched the side of the basin full of snow, they made a sharp noise as if they had been made of wood. After two hours of painful and slow treatment, movement came back to the fingers, but he did have to have four of them amputated and he lost the first half of two others. Had he gone on much longer without help, he would have lost both his hands.

Three weeks later, our poor mother could not dissimulate her suffering any more, and she had to admit that her resistance was gone. A tumour on the liver that had been operated on in 1899 must have caused new damages. At that time, X-rays were used only in Europe, and the only advice we had was that given by letter from Doctor Blais, in Edmonton, a French Canadian and a specialist. Naturally, he insisted that we take our mother to that city and the General Hospital on Victoria Avenue. Henri accompanied her.

When I saw the democrat turn slowly at the hill in front of the house, I had a premonition that something sad was going to happen. We received a telegram announcing that mother was to be operated on. Two days later, another one came to Big Valley, where a telegraph had been installed in the post office, with these words, "Operation a success. Patient doing well. Letter follows." Before we received the letter, a third telegram immediately summoned us to Edmonton.

I left with my father, who still seemed to be hopeful. When we entered the white-walled room, we saw at a glance that the end was near. Our poor father was heart-broken. Henri had to go back in order to help Jean, who had more work than he could do. Before we took leave of each other at the Strathcona Station on the south bank of the Saskatchewan, my brother said to me:

"I shall never see mother again. She has already left us. . . . Look after father well; . . . the poor man seems to have given up completely. What will her last moments be like for him? The doctor told me she would suffer greatly."

Upon my return to the hospital, I had all the trouble in the world sending father back to the hotel for a bit of rest. During the night, in spite of the morphine, the suffering was atrocious. At dawn, the Bishop came in to visit her, and, while the nurse was administering a needle, I accompanied the prelate, who said to me:

"My young friend, your mother is a saint. How resigned she is! What faith she has! I shall pray for her in a little while at mass."

Father came back at about the same time, and I was able to sleep a little. At ten-thirty in the morning, on 17 April, she passed away in my father's arms.

By a strange contrast, that very same day, spring broke out gloriously. Nature, which had been idle for the last five months, came out of its apparent death, . . . but death had just ravished from a husband and his children a person who was extremely gifted in all the best qualities of heart and soul.

In the cathedral in Edmonton, the hymns rose in their terrible majesty. Dr. Blais, two nuns, the nurse, my father, and myself, with the exception of the priest and the persons in the choir, were the only people present in the church . . . in this large, unknown city of Edmonton. At the end of the service, father, the priest, and I climbed into a horse-drawn cab and followed the coffin. Once out of Victoria Avenue and along Jasper Avenue, the two teams began to trot as street-cars and automobiles passed us on the asphalt streets (there were already numerous automobiles in Edmonton at the time). The people whom we saw did not pay any attention to our small cortege. We finally reached the Edmonton Catholic Cemetery and found it almost empty. Edmonton was still a young city then. There was a pile of rich earth by an open grave, next to another recently filled. I saw a name that appeared to be Slavic. In front was a small poplar bush whose leaves were soon to appear, and the birds were singing! Mother was there in the luxurious coffin. . . . After a murmur of prayers, we returned to the cab with a great emptiness in our hearts, . . . and I felt nauseated. We had to return to the hospital to get mother's belongings, and, as we left, I had to support my very unhappy father, who seemed completely lost.

The next day was again a very beautiful day. Spring was really here, and our distress seemed to count for so very little.

Upon our return to Stettler, we went to see Dr. Donovan. He was surprised at my father's reaction to his sorrow and advised him not to linger in places that had witnessed the last years of his life with mother. A complete diversion was necessary, such as a trip to France, for example. Father did not seem at all interested. All of this was of so little importance now. Once at home, however, before the pleading of his three sons, he made up his mind to follow our advice. We sold some cattle, prepared and cleaned the required clothing, checked his suits and shoes, and, on 3 May, Henri drove him to Stettler.

Two days later, around noon, while we thought that our traveller was on his way to Montreal to meet his old friend Musy, a rider from Big Valley brought us a laconic message from Dr. Blais, telling us that father was seriously ill at the hospital and that we should come as soon as possible. We were all completely stunned. Jean could not make up his mind whether or not to accompany Henri, and, even though my task was to look after the house, I decided to go. Naturally, it was at the hospital that we found out what was the matter.

As father was to spend a night in Edmonton on his way east, he got off the train at Strathcona and crossed the river to catch the CNR for Winnipeg, early the following morning. He had taken a room in the same hotel we had slept in previously. In the morning, he was unable to get up. An intense fever had completely drained him of his strength. The ambulance was called, and, father having been recognized, Dr. Blais was immediately alerted. He diagnosed bronchial pneumonia. The suffering and privations of the prisoner-of-war camps in Coblentz in 1871, the worries brought about by unsuccessful business ventures in France, the hard winter of 1906-07, and, especially, the recent loss of mother had probably counted for something in this crisis. He had no desire to live.

When we entered the room on the floor above the one where mother had been, we found him resigned and impassive. His face was calm and his eyes were closed. Henri approached and put his hand on father's shoulder, and he immediately opened his eyes. I said, rather loudly:

"Father, it's Henri and me, Marcel; . . . do you recognize us?"

He nodded his head and motioned for us to come closer.

"You want to tell us something?" asked Henri.

"Yes," he murmured. With a long pause between broken phrases, he said, "You had an admirable mother . . . I'm going to follow her. . . . Bishop came. . . . I'm at peace . . . you are able to manage. . . . Heaven will help you."

The doctor came in to see father, and he said in a rather loud voice:

"Medical science has done all it can; . . . when his heart gives out, it won't take long."

That night passed by slowly and without incident. Father was still in the same state. Henri had gone to rest at the hotel. Suddenly, I saw the hand resting on the side of the bed tremble slightly; . . . I felt that it was already cold; . . . the colour in his cheeks disappeared as if a curtain was being drawn, and that was all.

One hour later, Henri and I were seated facing each other in the next room, stunned and bewildered. We were very tired. The undertaker arrived, and, whether we wanted to or not, we had to accompany him to the funeral home in order to choose a coffin. All this array was hallucinating, and we chose one haphazardly. That night, we returned to the funeral parlour and saw our father lying there. I thought about the rough-hewn coffin of Father Laisnez . . . and the strange look in my mother's eyes!

The next morning, we were back at the cemetery. The undertaker had found a place next to mother's grave. I couldn't believe that only twenty-four days had gone by for all this to happen! The news of the double sorrow that afflicted us had spread among the French families of Edmonton, and, as I came out of the church, it seemed to me that I was shaking hands with thirty or more people. The same thing happened again at the cemetery.

That night, after having picked up father's things at the hospital, including his wallet, in which there was a large amount of money, we returned to the hotel and wrote letters. We had to let our friends in Canada and France know of our bereavement. When we went to bed, we went to sleep immediately.

In the middle of the night, Henri suddenly woke up. He remembered that he had left father's wallet on the desk in the lobby. We both dressed and went downstairs, but the night watchman told us we would have to wait until morning. We were at the desk when the day clerk came in. He motioned us into a small room and told us that he knew why we were there. Apparently, he knew the person who had the wallet, but that person wanted a large reward. We thought of calling the police, but the clerk seemed to think that it would be better for us to pay the man and recover our belongings than to create a whole lot of problems. Henri and I were so tired that we could not think clearly, and we agreed to this arrangement. Later, the wallet was returned, and, at least, we recovered part of the sum. How naive we had been!

Before taking our train at Strathcona, we spent some time walking along the majestic valley of the Saskatchewan

River. On its shores, imposing monuments were rising with the intention of lasting: the titanesque Parliament Buildings. The young capital of Alberta in this month of May 1910 was trembling with an impatient pride. It had great plans for the future; . . . everywhere, there was construction going on!

Upon our arrival at Stettler, we noticed that the flags were at half-mast. The king, Edward VII, had passed away. Friends were there to greet us, but I couldn't remember what they said. When we reached home, Jean appeared worried and too quiet. There were friends there, but, when they left, the three of us just sat without uttering a word.

The next morning, hunger ordered us to move. I took on my chores as housekeeper, but, each time I opened a cupboard door, memories rushed into my head. It wasn't time to dream anymore. We had to go on living in order for life to go on around us. The chickens were waiting, . . . the calves were bawling, . . . there were mountains of clothes to wash, and there was a lot of mending to do while my brothers were completing the seeding. One of the Laisnezs came to lend a hand. Boulot also showed up, and the de Bailleuxs, who this time were not quite so exuberant, and, finally, Father Renut, who came to spend a few days with us. He was worried about Jean, who had been talking strangely lately. Jean believed that he, too, had an internal tumour, and, to clear the air, we sent him to Edmonton. Henri and I had our suspicions that it was all in Jean's imagination and a result of the strain of the past few weeks. A letter from Dr. Blais led us to understand that our diagnosis was fairly correct, and, three weeks later, Jean returned a changed man, and the tremendous amount of work we had to do gradually began to heal our wounds.

IX

The difficulties of reaping

After successfully buying and selling cattle, our business prospered, and we were able to make the first down payment on the CPR half-section close to father and my quarters in the north. Those three-hundred-and-twenty acres were very rich land, and we had six years in which to pay. A Scottish settler, who owned three horses and a breaking plow, was hired to help us with the breaking. Seymour's house, which we had transported near to ours, became our Scotsman's home. At night, we all ate together.

A new French family had taken a half-section of homesteads on the other side of Big Valley, south-east of Lowden Lake. These new settlers came from Gennevilliers where they had been vegetable growers. So far, among the French settlers south of Stettler, the Parisian element of the French character had been missing, and all of us were happy to see the Pivert family adapt joyfully to their new life. In the family, there was a brother-in-law named Gabriel Basly, who was a bachelor. He offered to come and help us every weekend.

He would arrive on horseback on Friday nights, carrying an enormous pork roast, well seasoned and covered with gelatine; there was enough for all of us until Monday noon, including the Pivert family, which came to lunch on Sundays. In the afternoon, maman Pivert and her daughter mended, washed, and ironed clothes. When we had mass on Sundays, the Noullets would join the group and sleep over on Saturday nights. Papa Noullet had always kept his beard, and his little daughter, never having slept away from home and upon seeing

Jean lathering his face with a shaving brush, called her mother and, taking on a scandalized look, said:

"Mom, come and see Mr. Jean, who is washing his face with a little broom!"

The unchangeable rhythm of the seasons with their special tasks had made us forget our sorrow. The imperious obligation of accumulating a good provision of hay for the winter occupied us, and a new element of encouragement was being added: it was definite now that a railroad line would be built from Edmonton to Calgary via Stettler, Lowden Lake, and Big Valley, with a crossing of the Red Deer River at Tollman Creek. Three surveying crews had been out, and their three plans differed slightly, except with regard to Big Valley, where the topography did not allow for options. We were fairly sure, therefore, to get a station at Big Valley Post Office.

When the snow disappeared following the 1910-11 winter, the peaceful invasion of contractors and their crews began, and their caravans unfolded from north to south. At that time, all equipment had to be horse-drawn. The whole thing resembled a moving circus or a field battery. It was almost as if gold had been discovered and the gold rush was on. Many of these wagons were pulled by six teams. A military-type of discipline reigned everywhere, each one having his task to perform and not wasting time. The authorities, having finally established the route to be followed, had given each gang the task of building the roadway for half a mile. There were usually ten such gangs working simultaneously, so that, normally, the work spread out over five miles.

Canvas towns went up, with their stables, dining rooms, sleeping quarters, kitchens, blacksmith shops, stores, etc. The shares of special breaking plows were sharpened on anvils, and many were required each day. There were six horses hitched to what we might call the ancestor of the steam shovel. This, in turn, was followed by three plows that bit into the hill to be levelled, digging furrows one yard wide and ten inches deep. Immediately behind, the scrapers took action. An enormous shovel, pulled by four horses and able to carry one-third of a cubic yard, was set up on wheels so it would tilt. A lever action from the back lowered the cutting edge of the shovel so that it would bite into the soil. When the scraper was full, one of the two teams was unhooked and the other team did the hauling. The unhooked team was then hitched to the following scraper. The load was, in turn, dumped on top of the grade. All of this constituted some sort of endless chain, without any false manoeuvres. From morning until noon, the hill was completely gouged out, and, in the depression, a roadbed filled the swamp that had been there for millions of years! Only large stumps or rocks slowed down the operation, . . . and, then, the dynamite entered into play.

On a flat surface, such as that of Big Valley, the work progressed rapidly. Two thicknesses of furrows would dig the ditches, yielding enough dirt for a roadway one yard high. This would allow the winter winds to sweep the snow off the tracks. Between the Battle and the Red Deer Rivers, small bridges were built on pilings. From one week to the next, camps moved as other sections were started, and, one day, all of these sections were joined together. The crews left, and as we went to Big Valley to get our mail, the countryside was empty once again. There was only the grade inscribing the mark of civilization by its rectilinear lines and graceful curves. Rain, frost, and thaw were going to raise, pack, or dig into this soil ripped from its original state; next year, a track grader would come along and the ties and rails would be laid, . . . and trains would run.

In the meantime, our harvest was cut. We now had about two hundred acres in crops. Twenty huge stacks could be seen in groups of four along the high stubble where plows were once more tracing their furrows. All around us, farmers had done as we did, so threshing crews were in demand. October was ending, and the days were frightfully short; sometimes a straw stack was set on fire so that a farmer's field could be finished that night. Winter was pressing on. In the morning, ice formed on the edges of the sloughs, . . . and, as a preface to so many others, the first blizzard roared ceaselessly for two days and three nights, leaving snowbanks three feet high before the calm returned. Threshing outfits gave in, one by one, but, in our isolated corner, the crews were miles away from us. If we didn't take action, we were going to face a disaster, because the fine powdered snow, pushed by strong winds, would find its way right into the sheaves of the stack, and, in the spring, water would spoil our grain.

North of Ewing, however, there was a crew still operating, who were reputed to be tough, but that was fifteen

miles away and the terrain was rough. The owner of the threshing outfit was ready to help us, but he needed an extra twelve
horses to help pull the outfit through, the thresher wheels being
mounted on skids.

We organized the expedition. Neighbours supplied
nine horses, and we threw in our three. On the way, we picked
up a sleigh and a team at the Harringtons' to haul supplies for
men and animals. Finally, the de Bailleuxs, who had a small
crop that year, lent two horses to haul the water for the boiler.

When we left the next morning at dawn, the weather
was beautiful. At first, we crossed a rather flat region; the
steam engine, using its large wheels, flattened the snow in front
of our horses, which were pulling the threshing machine. We
moved at two miles an hour without incident, but, after two
hours, the steam engine had already devoured the wood pile and
we had to go out in search of more fuel. In an overflow of Ewing
Lake, we found some dead wood. By this time, it was four
o'clock and almost dark. The tractor moved onto the ice of the
lake. . . . Was it going to stand all this weight? We left a few
hundred yards between the engine and us before venturing on
the ice with the thresher. Suddenly, there was a detonation like
a cannon shot, and a crack travelling at the speed of lightning
moved across the lake. . . . It wasn't serious. A little water
appeared, and the air which had been compressed between the
water and the ice was suddenly released as the engine passed
over the pocket. Now, the ice was resting everywhere on the
water, and there was no more danger.

As the moon was well over the first quarter, we
continued in the dark for six more kilometres and stopped the
convoy by the river bank, where there were numerous dead
trees. We immediately started to saw them in order to keep the
boiler alive all night and the pressure up; it was twenty-five
below zero, and, had we not done this, the boiler would have
split before morning. While we were busy sawing trees, others
were taking care of the horses. There was a new stable at this
location, and the boss had chosen the spot on purpose. The
engineer and his son had installed a temporary kitchen and
prepared an unbelievable supper, which we swallowed heartily.
We then rolled up in our blankets and slept, almost under the
horses!

Before dawn, the engineer let out a blast of the engine's

whistle that echoed across the frozen lake. Until daybreak, and for part of the morning, we moved with difficulty because of the small hills in the area; our vehicle kept sliding. In the huge snowbanks, the tractor would invariably get stuck, its enormous wheels spinning and sliding on the spot. Again, as always, the horses were called upon to pull out the machines. On the slopes, it was the thresher that started to slip sideways down the hill, and four horses had to be hooked to its side to put it back on track. Going downhill, things went much more easily, the engineer knowing all the tricks for braking during the descent.

We stopped to eat in the shelter of the machines. We fueled the engine and were on our way again, but not for long. Snow had begun to fall, and the wind increased rapidly. At three o'clock, although it was already half dark, we struggled on until we arrived at the spot below the de Bailleuxs', where, five years ago, we had had to criss-cross so many times.

Five years, . . . and it was still the same rugged life; the endless struggle for survival!

The wood ran out, and nobody had the courage to go out and fetch some. The engineer emptied the boiler, and, tomorrow, in order to build up pressure, we would have to heat for three hours. We had only one thing in mind, . . . to warm up, eat, and sleep.

Nobody moved the next morning. Even the horses were lying in their stalls. Hubert de Bailleux made a huge pot of coffee and looked very gloomy. Somehow, I got the message that he wasn't at all in favour of the machines going any farther. I found the engineer in the hayloft and bluntly asked him if we were going to carry on. He replied:

"See the boss! If the horses move, I'll move."

The boss had gone out to see a friendly neighbour, and his foreman told me that he, personally, wouldn't mind, although he hoped we wouldn't break any essential parts. I could see his point. I then attempted to persuade the drivers. Here, I met more resistance, but, by appealing to their spirit of sportsmanship, I succeeded.

Back to the wood pile and the water-tank! By eleven o'clock, we were on our way for the last lap. The whistle blasted again, as if defying all the hills around that separated us from our goal. It had snowed during the night, but, the wind having died down, the new snow helped the traction of the metal wheels so that we arrived without incident at the home of the first farmer on this run who was to use the machine.

For ten days, this infernal work, painful enough in good weather, went on in the wind, cold, and snow. As ice accumulated inside the water-tank, it held less and less water and more and more trips were needed to keep the boiler happy. Another gang spent its time sawing wood to keep the fire alive night and day. We certainly did earn those bushels of wheat sold the following spring, . . . and the English ladies who made muffins or pancakes never suspected, I am sure, all the effort that had gone into them.

X

The first train in Big Valley

The year 1912 was introduced in the traditional way: snowstorms and severe low temperatures. Our morale was boosted by the acquisition of a gramophone and fifty well-chosen records. This marvelous invention, which, for its time, had almost attained perfection, allowed us to participate in the audition of masterpieces of music and song. Lost as we were in snowstorms, all that was required was to imagine ourselves among the audience of great concerts given by the most famous orchestras or the most reputed singers. Later, each time we could, we improved our collection by purchasing the latest recordings and classical pieces. I sometimes thought how our parents would have enjoyed listening to these. . . .

In the spring, rumour had it that the bridge over the Battle River had been finished. This had been the principal obstacle between the Red Deer River and Edmonton. One morning, while in Stettler, where I had spent the night, I heard repeated whistle blasts coming from the north. This whistle did not sound like the one on the CPR whose echo always came from the east or west of the station. A large cloud of steam and smoke rose in spurts toward the sky; . . . the gang of men who set the railroad ties was approaching.

Then, the big bell on the locomotive began ringing, . . . to which the town church bells echoed along with the school bell. Like ants on the march, the tie carriers, two by two followed each other in Indian file; they dropped their load in its place, and two other men with picks straightened it out. Every twenty feet, there were thirty ties set down; they came off rolling hooks in front of the first wagon as a second one got into place. At the same time, the rails were placed on the positioned ties by pulleys. The mobile spacers, one in front, one in the middle, and one at the back, covered the rails as the diabolical crew of spike drivers entered into play. These enormous nails hooked the rail onto the tie. A first man, kneeling, gave the first hammer blow, and the others were given by two spike drivers, who pounded them down in a rhythmic full swing of the long hammer. In an infernal noise of twenty hammers falling and bouncing, we could see the spikes disappear into the wood of the tie. At the same time, the fish-plates were set in their places under the distributor car.

Some gentlemen, dressed for the occasion, were standing by the seven-year-old CPR line. Another similar group came up from the approaching convoy. There were mutual handshakes. Then, the boss brought out a large nickel-coated chisel and a bronzed hammer with a mahogany handle. While he held on to the chisel, these gentlemen, each in turn, gave it a blow with the hammer. More handshakes followed and the ceremony was over. The friendly crossing of two competing companies was established. The minute cut would be properly gouged later; but, for today, the rails were elevated a little so that the wheels could easily pass over the other rails.

Seventeen days later, while work was progressing rapidly on the bridge over the Red Deer at Tollman Creek, the rail crew arrived at Big Valley, and it was learned that a round-house would be built there—to the great dismay of people in Stettler. Another crew had left Calgary, and, when it reached the Red Deer from the south, it carried with it the steel beams for the bridge, which had come from the United States. In September, the first train rolled from Edmonton to Calgary via Big Valley.

During the winter, towns sprouted all along the railroad at intervals of seven or eight miles. For us, they were Lowden Lake, Big Valley, Scollard, and Drumheller. Big Valley was nine miles away, Scollard, seven and a half, and Drumheller, fifteen. The railroad that followed Big Valley made a huge circle, and we were in the middle of the circumference.

In mid-October, we were able to haul wheat to Scollard; we could make two trips a day with two wagons, the Laisnezs providing us with a helper. The following spring, we were allowed one wagonload of wheat at the Big Valley elevator. The town took on new importance as a railroad centre where crews changed. It was the mid-point between Calgary and Edmonton. A very comfortable hotel had been built, which was operated by a compatriot of Bonnevie, a Belgian by the name of François Rentiers, an excellent man who became a link between all the French-speaking people in the area. He would take the parcels from the station and would also expedite some; he also sent urgent mail. A coal mine operated by professionals had been opened up, and, in spite of the distance, we preferred loading here from the pile than take the risks we had taken.

A branch of the Merchant's Bank, opened at first only three days a week, was provided, then, a Chinese restaurant and cleaning service, a pool hall, a general store with hardware and farm implements, a blacksmith shop with livery barn, and, finally, a post office, which had a telephone.

The rail traffic consisted at first of one mixed train in each direction. One year later, a short passenger train allowed us to go and return from Stettler the same day. What used to take seven or eight hours by wagon could now be accomplished in a little over one and a half hours!

That year, after the threshing season, Henri went to the old country to get married. My older brother, Jean, decided to leave the Durieux Brothers Society to become the associate of a young Frenchman named Coiffard, with the intention of staying on his own farm after the winter. In the meantime, Coiffard and Jean went to Europe to buy an Ardennois stallion. They wanted to start a new race of horses in the region. I was left alone and had received instructions from Henri to plaster the interior of the house while he was away.

I called on the Lourdels, where I knew that Siméon and his father were not getting along too well. Upon my return from Stettler with the plaster laths, we proceeded to nail them all over the walls so that the plaster could take hold. I had been given the address of a plasterer who lived somewhere near Lethbridge and who was convalescing at a friend's home in Tail Creek, the station before Stettler. I went there and found a short man who looked tired and weak. He accepted my offer, and, for fear of losing him, I took him back with me.

The first question the plasterer asked me, as he took a

look at the work we had done, was whether or not there was a cellar in the house. . . . I understood him to mean liquor, wine, etc., . . . and, as I talked, I saw his face light up. He somehow reminded me of Foot, the carpenter, when we brought out the bottle of whisky. However, the plasterer needed sand, that was why he had asked the question, and sand was easy to obtain in the cellar.

Once the furniture was removed from the room, we went to work. I mixed the plaster in a huge trough in the kitchen; . . . it was much too cold outside. The work progressed rapidly. This little fellow, in spite of his peaked appearance, had a surprising capacity for work. The difficult operation required in order to plaster the ceiling seemed a game to him. After the noon meal the following day, I noticed that he felt drowsy; . . . I thought about the bottle of whisky, . . . and lo and behold! It worked! By a clever dosage of the liquid, I was able to get the first coat put on, the second one to be applied one week later. However, a few days later I saw a cutter, in which there were three persons, coming down the hill, and someone waving at me. It was the newlyweds, who were arriving home sooner than expected.

The new Mrs. Durieux showed her mettle by taking a scraper and cleaning the floor of her room! We moved the furniture back, and, at night, the room really looked good, . . . although a little damp. My sister-in-law, Marguerite, was a tall and beautiful woman who was well able to take on her new tasks. She adapted very quickly to this rough life and to the cold winter now in full force.

Jean and his friend also returned, but without the stallion. Apparently, it would not have endured the ocean crossing. The house, which had been empty three weeks ago, was now over-populated, and so, once again, the winter passed without incident.

In the precocious early spring of 1913 we heard that friends and relatives of Marguerite had arrived and were looking for land in the south-east. By that time, Jean and Coiffard had built their house, and, when these relatives arrived, we took two of them apiece. They loved our company so much that they stayed until fall! On the eve of their departure, we received a telegram announcing that Marguerite's father was seriously ill in France. She joined the group of her relatives, who, after having spent the summer with us, had finally decided to go back home.

I returned to my "house-keeping" tasks until my sister-in-law's return in the month of March 1914. After her departure, her father's health had improved; however, ten days after her return, a telegram announced the death of Mr. Mairesse.

This fatal year began with more bad news. In Canada, we felt that war was at hand, ... perhaps more so than in France where Germany's declaration that she would not recognize Belgian neutrality in case of war had taken the French by surprise. We read the *Courrier des Etats-Unis*, a French newspaper printed in New York, by Frenchmen, which kept us informed.

That year, part of our crop had been damaged by frost. We fed some of the grain to our cattle, and, when they were ready, with the de Bailleuxs we drove both our herds to the stock-yards at Tail Creek. Upon our return, the de Bailleuxs decided to celebrate the sale by preparing a huge rum omelette.

Hubert had decided that this was going to be a masterpiece. He broke twenty eggs into a big salad bowl and poured two glasses of rum into the mixture, while Joseph, having tasted the preparation and found it tasteless, took advantage of a moment when Hubert's back was turned to pour in the rest of the bottle.

As the omelette cooked, Hubert's nostrils kept on dilating, and, when he sat down to eat, he muttered:

"Well I'll be damned! I would never have thought that the rum in the dark bottle was so strong!"

All of us took small portions of the omelette, which served as an "entre-mets," while we kept coaxing Hubert.

"Come on, Hubert. We thought you were starved. You can finish it!"

"That's right, I am starved, and I'm not going to let this go to waste. You know, this is really a very good omelette!"

A few minutes later, our friend, who was naturally exuberant, became so loquacious that he forgot to smoke! He turned his high spirits toward me.

"Well now, my little Marcel (I was fifteen centimetres taller than he was, but, from the very first day and for eight years, he always referred to me as little Marcel), now that Henri is married, it's your turn next! For example, there's the young Randon girl; she's only seventeen, but who knows . . . in a year or so she might be very receptive. . . ."

"Oh! Oh! That's maybe what you think, but there is young Fournier who is interested, and he's building a house! That's a pretty good sign. All the bachelors are invited for a housewarming on 14 July. What if it were a stag?"

The unfortunate Fournier would not take Claire Randon as his wife. Two months later, it would be a Lebel gun with fixed bayonet that was placed in his hands, . . . and he would be the first one, of the French contingent of Lowden Lake called to arms, to fall, on 18 September on the Chemin des Dames at the end of the Battle of the Marne.

But, that's another story. . . .

Epilogue

On 31 July 1974, in a special edition of the *Big Country News*, commemorating Big Valley's sixtieth anniversary, there appeared a short article on the Durieux family, written by Marcel Durieux, then eighty-two years of age. In this article, Marcel describes the events that followed the outbreak of World War I and what happened to himself and his two brothers.

Jean and Marcel left Big Valley in the summer of 1914 for France; there Marcel enlisted in the Foreign Legion and Jean, a sergeant in the reserve, rejoined his regiment. Henri followed them a few months later and joined the field artillery, in which he won the Croix de Guerre as well as the Military Medal, which was presented to him by the Duke of Connaught. Jean became an officer and lost his life in action during the Battle of Verdun in 1916. Henri returned to Big Valley in 1918 to rejoin his wife. After her death in 1931, he married Alice Depelchin; from this marriage, a daughter, Jeanne, was born. Jeanne is now married to Bert Golosky of Fort McMurray, Alberta, and the couple have six daughters. Marcel, having suffered from an attack of poison gas during the war, was unable to return to Canada because of his poor health. He settled at Iteuil (Vienne), France, where he passed away on 29 June 1976.

The beginning of the Great War in 1914 affected many of the French settlers in Alberta. Although Canada was their adopted land, they heard the cry for help from France, and they went back, sorrowfully but without hesitation. Many of them lost their lives or had their health so affected that they were unable to return to the arduous life of a pioneer Alberta farm. The result was that, at a critical time in the development of the province, many of its strong, young settlers were suddenly snatched away, thus depriving the land of precisely the sort of people it most greatly needed.

However, the extraordinary sacrifices of these first settlers were not made in vain. Today, many of those communities that they helped settle and open to agriculture are flourishing. Thus, the names and the work of these pioneers are not completely forgotten. It is hoped that the publication of this manuscript will also help to keep their memory alive.